Human Evolution Cookbook

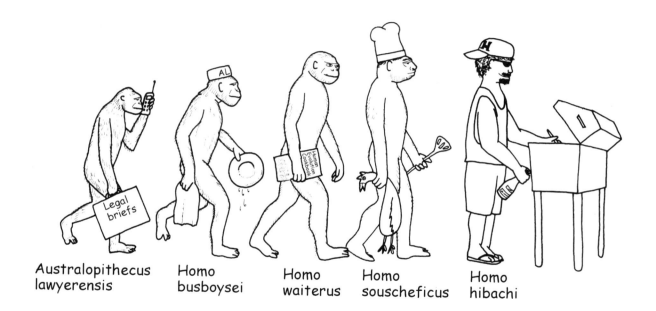

Australopithecus lawyerensis

Homo busboysei

Homo waiterus

Homo souscheficus

Homo hibachi

Human Evolution Cookbook

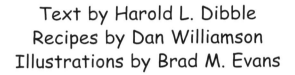

Text by Harold L. Dibble
Recipes by Dan Williamson
Illustrations by Brad M. Evans

University of Pennsylvania Museum
of Archaeology and Anthropology

Library of Congress Cataloging-in-Publication Data
Dibble, Harold Lewis.
The human evolution cookbook:
text by Harold L. Dibble;
recipes by Dan Williamson;
illustrations by Brad M. Evans.
p. cm.
ISBN 1-931707-49-9
1. Human evolution – Popular works.   I. Williamson, Dan.   II. Title.
GN281 .D53 2003
599.93'8–dc21   2002155090

CONTENTS

Recipes

Preface

The idea to do a book combining a dash of prehistory, a sprinkle of recipes, and a generous helping of humor came about some years ago during the excavation of one of our Paleolithic sites in southern France. Dan has been our project cook for a number of years and is, therefore, one of the most important people on our excavations. Besides fixing absolutely stunning food (we boast frequently that we're the only archaeological project that serves soufflé!), he also manages the camp, runs errands for the students, and plays a nice guitar. Brad, another fine guitar player, has done many of our lithic (stone tool) illustrations and other kinds of artwork for some of our publications and websites.   His own work, for the Bernice P. Bishop Museum in Hawai'i, is also first rate.

Although the book does present a basically factual outline of the major accomplishments over the past four million years or so, it is not written to teach anyone about human evolution. It does identify some of the major players and it also focuses heavily on some of the current debates that are taking place. Let's just say that it tries to present some information on human evolution in a more palatable form, but readers who wish to know more "facts" should definitely consult any of a number of books that are written for the lay public. And if anyone wants to know what I really think about the subject, then they should definitely consult my scholarly publications and not try to interpret what I've written here. Above all, it has been a lot of fun for the three of us to collaborate on something that is not really work—poking fun of one's own discipline is definitely not work—and we hope that the reader enjoys it as well.

Our thanks to the many people—Museum staff, students, and colleagues—who have read the text and tried the recipes. Of course, they assume no responsibility for your own tastes in either humor or food.

Food and Evolution

As a professor of archaeology, I'm often asked two things. The first question, and by far the most common one, is "Uh, do I have to know that for the final exam?" The second question, which usually comes from a more diverse group of strangers and a seemingly unending line of distant relatives who come to visit us, is "How did humans evolve?" It's my nature as an educator that whenever I'm confronted by someone who is really curious about things and who wants to learn, I immediately assume my "Professorial mode" and reply, "That's a very complex question. When did you say you were leaving?"

And it *is* a complex question. If it weren't, there would be no need for people like me to spend all their lives digging up completely useless bits of broken stones and bones—and get paid for doing it! In order to answer it, I first have to give a little background as to how evolution works.

We've all heard the phrase "survival of the fittest," which most people believe is one of the underlying principles of evolution. Actually, this phrase doesn't have much to do with the theory of evolution, but rather was invented to help explain why people like Jane Fonda and Richard Simmons seem to be around bothering the rest of us for a very, very long time. No—evolution is not a question of exercise and being fit. Evolution is really much better than that since it involves the one thing that's on everyone's mind, namely SEX. Now that you realize that this book is much more interesting than any ordinary cookbook, you should go ahead and buy it so that you can continue reading it at home.

1

So, as I was saying, evolution involves sex. Some readers are going to realize immediately the single most important implication of that statement, namely that Charles Darwin was not the stuffy old man that most people think—he actually had a life! And it was during a certain climactic moment of his life that he realized that the important thing about evolution was to produce offspring. OK, it's true that Darwin was more concerned with finches and turtles than people (his life wasn't that interesting), but what else do you do when you're stuck on an island in the middle of nowhere? The idea is this: if you have children, then they will pass on your jeans (spelled *g-e-n-e-s*) to their children, and so on through the generations. In a sense, you will keep on living, thanks to your children and grandchildren. There is a certain irony to this in that most of us feel that life came to an abrupt end when we had kids.

Now, as every adolescent knows, the hard part is to live long enough to start having sex. And that's where the word "adaptation" comes in. If you're well adapted (which is different than being well adjusted) then you'll eventually reach that magic moment. If you're not well adapted—if you're doing things that will lead to your early death—then it's too bad for you and for the evolution thing, at least as far as your line is concerned.

"OK," you say, "I understand that in order to have sex I have to be well adapted. But what does being well adapted really mean?" Well, if you think about it, the answer is easy. To keep living and eventually grow up, you've got to eat. If you don't eat, you can't possibly live long enough to have sex and pass along your genes to the next generation. You may do everything else perfectly, but if what you're doing doesn't result in an adequate intake of calories, you're history (or prehistory, as they used to call it before writing was developed). An evolutionary dead-end. So, it's like what the French have always understood—food and sex together are the two most important things in life, or in this case, evolution.

That small digression finally brings us back to the question of how did we evolve (I warned you that it was a complex question). The answer, however, is simple: We did it by eat-

2

Homo habilis   Homo erectus   Homo sapiens

ing. Which is where this book comes in, though those of you who happened to pay attention to the title already figured that part out. For the rest of you, I'll just say that this book is all about how our prehistoric ancestors adapted by developing wholesome and m'm m'm good things to eat.

Before we get going, some of you may have some questions. For example, many readers will ask, "Am I going to be able to believe any of the stuff that's in this book?" Well, that depends. I will be willing to guarantee that when it comes to the accounts dealing with the various prehistoric periods, everything that I write will be the absolute truth. Of course, as we've learned already from our politicians, there's nothing absolute about truth—it's all relative and based on how you wish to define your terms. So, let's just say that all of the prehistory that's presented here will reflect either my understanding of it, or at least my opinions about it, except for the parts that I make up for the sake of keeping your interest. As for Chef Dan's recipes, they are honest-to-God recipes, based on real food items, and they are fully digestible (well, maybe). Whether or not they actually help you to pass along your genes—well, that's another thing altogether. But, hey—good luck.

And finally, I'm sure that some reader is going to ask: "Look, I just bought this @#&! book because earlier you said that it was going to be about sex! Now you're telling me it's about food. What's up with that?" I've got an answer for that too: "Ha-ha—too late! We don't offer refunds."

The Earliest Humans

Several million years ago some furry ape took that first big step and then promptly fell from a tree with a resounding thud. Embarrassing? Of course. But it started us down the long road toward something that we might call human. Exactly when that point was reached depends on what you mean by that term. Let's make it clear right away that deciding on what is human is very difficult—I have plenty of academic colleagues (especially deans and related forms of single-brain-celled organisms) for whom I would never use their name and the word "human" in the same sentence. But most paleoanthropologists (which can mean either someone who studies prehistoric human evolution or simply any anthropologist who is extremely old) tend to agree that one characteristic is very important in defining the initial threshold: bipedalism (or walking upright on two legs). This appears to have developed in East Africa about 4.5 million years ago.

Of course, some people would argue that bipedalism is not absolutely necessary to be human. But after watching the Philadelphia Eagles offensive line (a very appropriate term, I might add) for a number of years, I'm personally convinced that those who spend too much time crouched with their knuckles on the ground are not exactly like the rest of us.

Anyway, there are two extraordinary finds that have come to light for this earliest time of humanity. The first was by Professor Donald Johanson in 1974 of a number of human remains in Ethiopia, including one named "Lucy" (aka *Australopithecus* [ahs-trail-o-PITH-ikus] *afarensis* [a, as in absolutely-far-EN-sis], roughly translated as "a pithy-brained ape-like creature who could walk a far ways, even to Australia, assuming she could read a map"). Lucy was a young individual when she died, which probably means that she didn't have much of an opportunity to pass

Hadar Fossils

Reconstructions

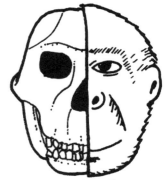

Johanson and White, 1973

Schultz, 1952

along her own genes. But even so, we know from studying her bones that she was bipedal, which puts her right up there with the rest of us in the walking department. On the other hand, she was no real winner in the brains department (having a brain only slightly larger than that of a chimpanzee). The lack of so-called grey matter (that is, the squishy stuff that's inside your head) may explain why Lucy and her relatives had not yet discovered how to make even the simplest of stone tools or to use fire. Nonetheless, Lucy has achieved a great deal of notoriety, which goes to show that in the fossil world just being in the right place at the right time is more important than having any sort of skill or intelligence. I'm referring, of course, to the paleoanthropologists who make these sorts of discoveries, not to our ancient ancestors.

Even more remarkable was the discovery in Tanzania by the late Dr. Mary Leakey at the site of Laetoli (pronounced lay-TOE-lee, for reasons which will be obvious in a second) of a trail of footprints preserved in a layer of volcanic ash. Along a distance of about 20 meters are two sets of prints, one belonging to an older person and one set belonging to a child. The most important implications of this find are (1) people then spent a lot of time hiking; and (2) shoes had not been invented yet. Parents should take note also that it may not be a good idea to clean up when your kids track mud inside—those footprints may be worth bazillions some day in the future.

This leaves certain questions unanswered, though. For one, why did Lucy and her relatives start walking around on two feet to begin with? The answer is not at all obvious, especially when you consider that most of our modern back problems are a result of this new-fangled mode of locomotion. The trouble is that our backbones are not designed to keep all that weight (OK, I'll be honest—all my weight) in a vertical position all the time. But the plus side of walking on two feet is that you only have to buy half as many shoes and after a long day out on the trail you won't have stinky hands. Some people think that the sole reason, so to speak, was to free up our hands for doing other things—carrying objects, for example, or maybe making obscene gestures. The point is, maybe it wasn't the fact that we walked on two feet that was so

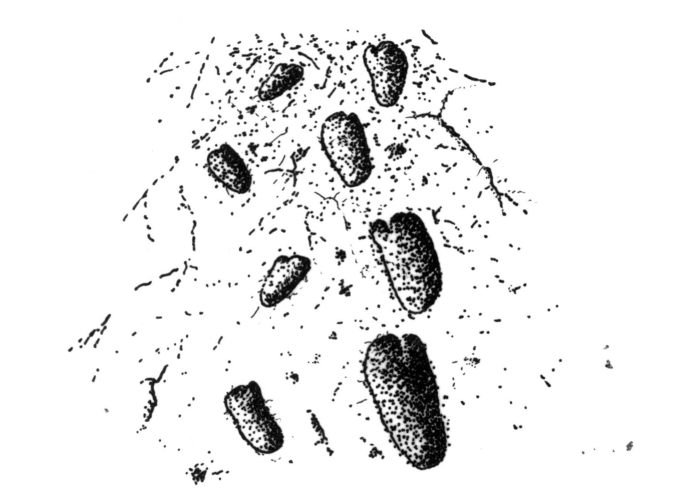

important, but rather that by doing so we got to evolve a whole new set of hands. This means that the real breakthrough was bihandedness, not bipedality, which ultimately led to things like being able to use typewriters and knitting needles effectively.

Let me make clear that we don't know for sure that Lucy and her gang were the first bihanded hominids (hominid is science-talk for early humans). As we speak, there are many dedicated teams of intrepid explorers scouring the plains of East Africa looking for even older scraps of bone that would allow them (the fossil hunters) to claim that they found the earliest one. That's what archaeology is all about—find the oldest and you become famous (until someone else finds something earlier).

Besides, if you find some new kind of fossil you get to assign a new name to it, much to the delight of anthropology students everywhere who have to learn how to spell it. Most people don't realize that there are certain rules about naming fossils. First of all, the name has to be somehow related to Latin, which basically means that it has to end with "us" or "ens" or "is." This is intended to make it sound more "scientific." The New York Times, for example, would refuse to believe the validity of some new fossil called Australopithecus bob. Naming it Australopithecus robertensis, on the other hand, would guarantee front-page coverage in the Science section. Second, it helps if you build the new name so that it includes the name of some rich donor. So, for example, if I found an important new fossil, I wouldn't feed my own ego by naming it Australopithecus dibblus, but rather Australopithecus donandbettyjonesensis. This helps to keep the money flowing in, which is a lot more important than ego.

Speaking of ego, it should be said that the dedicated scientists making all of these fantastic early hominid discoveries are probably the most humble of all paleoanthropologists. But since I promised not to make too many things up, I won't actually say that.

Anyway, let's get back to what this book is all about. Without tools and without fire, it is clear that the diet back in the dawn of humanity was not spectacular. What was needed was food that was portable and could be replenished as you walked along. So, after careful study, Chef Dan has developed the Laetoli Trail Mix. This is so good that it is sure to have hikers of any time period (even small-brained Australopithecines) hooting for more.

Study Questions

1. If walking on two feet is a sign of humanness, why aren't chickens considered human?
2. If the Philadelphia Eagles actually won the Super Bowl (yeah, right—look, I said "if") would they be considered human? Explain why or why not.
3. Name five things that you can do with your hands that you cannot (or would not) do with your feet? Would any of these things help you to pass along your genes to the next generation?

10

Laetoli Trail Mix

1-1/2 cups rolled oats
1/2 cup toasted almonds (any nuts will do here, but I like almonds)
1/2 cup shredded coconut
1/4 cup bran
1/4 cup melted butter
1/4 cup honey
1 tsp. vanilla extract
1 cup raisins and other dried fruit mixed together
   (I like dried papaya and apricots, but you may find pineapple
   to your liking or any other dried fruit you can find lying
   around in your neighborhood)

   Preheat oven to 350 degrees.
   Mix the oats, almonds, coconut, and bran together in a big
bowl. Melt the butter and honey together in a pan. Add the vanilla
and remove from heat. Pour over the dried ingredients and mix
together. Bake on a cookie sheet until golden brown, about 30
minutes, stirring every 5-10 minutes to prevent burning. Mix the
fruit into the granola while it cools. Store in a tight sealing
container. It is enough for about 10 people unless you eat like Jethro
Bodine.

Lucy's Legumes

Fresh vegetables—carrots, celery, peppers, broccoli, cauliflower, etc.
16-oz. container of sour cream
1 packet French onion soup mix
1 lb. fresh spinach or 1 small package of frozen spinach

Lucy and her crowd were probably not big meat eaters, so this might be a dish to serve when your own hunt is unsuccessful. The first thing you need to do is to go out and gather some vegetables. The kinds you get are going to depend on where you live in the world, or what your grocery store carries. I like to cut these into julienne strips, pieces about 1/8 of an inch on each side and about 2 inches long. In other words, bite sized. Now, the French like to do what we call blanching the vegetables, which is to dunk them into boiling water for a short time and then dunk them into ice water to stop the cooking process. This softens them a bit and sets the color. I prefer this method, though it is more common in America to leave them raw. I believe Lucy would have had them this way since her brain was too small to use fire.

(continued on next page)

12

The next thing is to get some sour cream and one of those dried packets of French onion soup mix. I make this a little different where I work, but to simplify, one of these packets will work nicely. Make sure it has freeze-dried onions in it. Mix enough of it with the sour cream to suit your taste. Take the fresh spinach and pull the stems off. Then put about a tablespoon of oil (I like olive oil but any vegetable oil will do) into a sauté pan and heat it up. Put in the spinach to wilt it. This will only take about 30 seconds or so. Cool and add it to the dip. If you are using frozen spinach you will just need to thaw and drain most of the liquid before adding to the dip. This will make a nice dip for your favorite legumes.

  If you hate vegetables (as it seems so many people do), then you can get one of those round pumpernickel loaves and hollow it out. Save the pieces you take out to dunk into the dip. Then put the dip into the bread bowl and arrange the pieces around it on a tray. You can enjoy it this way, too.

Oldowan Chopper Diagnostic Analysis

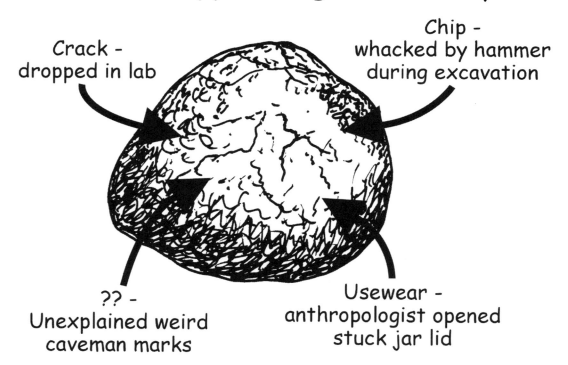

Crack - dropped in lab

Chip - whacked by hammer during excavation

?? - Unexplained weird caveman marks

Usewear - anthropologist opened stuck jar lid

The First Tool-Makers

About 2.5 million years ago early humans started making the first stone tools. Now, when I say "tool" you should not think of some complicated, testosterone-dripping, Tim Allen-kind of device. No, the first tools were not like that at all. Quite literally, the first tools were simply broken rocks. Yes, that's right—broken rocks. But even so, these simple things laid the foundation for all of the rest of mankind's great technological achievements, eventually leading to the ultimate in prisoner labor and the Rolling Stones, who some would argue is rock's greatest achievement. I personally prefer the Beatles.

Now, I suppose you're wondering how a broken rock could serve as a tool. Some of you may be saying that it could be used as a hammer, but keep in mind that nails (other than the ones found on your fingers and toes) were not invented yet. We could throw a rock, and maybe bring down a giant mammoth (please don't try that on your own). But in either case a whole, unbroken rock would serve perfectly well in that capacity (in fact, even wild chimpanzees use rocks or logs as hammers to crack nuts open).

The fact is that many kinds of rocks, when struck in a certain way, will break so that the small bits that come off (which are called flakes) are virtually razor sharp. Assuming that you don't cut off a finger or put out your eye first, these flakes can be used as knives to cut up even the toughest antelope or any other big creature you might feel like eating. These flakes can also be easily shaped into various specialized forms, like scrapers or arrowheads (though the first arrowheads didn't appear until millions of years later). So, rocks broken in a certain way can be very useful.

Making stone tools is a lot harder than it looks. Oh, wait—you probably don't even know what it looks like to make them. Well, picture this: you first pick up a rock and hold it in one hand. Then pick up a second rock with the other hand. Then you hit one rock against the other hard enough that one of them breaks. Yes, I'm sure that in your mind's eye it looks so easy that any moron could do it, but believe me, it is … well, it's … uh …. ok, ok, ok—any moron could do it. But what's interesting is that chimpanzees cannot do it, at least very well. One of my colleagues, Dr. Nick Toth, has spent several years trying to teach a chimp named Kanzi to make stone tools, and while he (Kanzi) seems to enjoy bashing things together, the results are not as sophisticated as even the earliest stone tools we find in the archaeological record.   So there.

So, our earliest stone tool–making ancestors were better than chimps, but nonetheless the tools they made were still not very complicated. Anyway, that fact doesn't make these tools any less important as a major technological milestone on the great highway of humanity. In fact, it's the most important thing ever. To understand why, you have to know a few things. The first is that another word for stone tools is lithics. Second, what most people call the Old Stone Age is also known as the Paleolithic period. Third, I am a Paleolithic archaeologist. So, without stone tools, there would be no Paleolithic and I would not have anything to study. This makes the invention of stone tools critically important to me. Of course, I would still have my job, since there are many in academe who get along fine without any actual subject matter.

But stone tools are important for other reasons as well, and again I'm going to call upon your imagination here to fill in the picture. First of all, take a careful look at what wimps these early hominids were. Let's see—they were furry, stood about four feet tall, with no claws, fangs, or poisonous stingers. Oh, and they weren't that bright, either. Is this the kind of "person" who is going to be able to ravage their environment to suit their will, savagely hunt big game to

Flake Typology

Basalt

Flint

Coconut

Corn

Dandruff

Ziggy

extinction, attack their neighbors without provocation, and do all the other things we consider to be major hallmarks of humanity? No, of course not.

Now, picture this same individual with a broken rock in his or her hand. The picture changes, doesn't it? Imagine him delicately slicing open mammoths, giant sloths, woolly hippos, and other Ice Age beasts with a flake rather than trying to tear it apart with his bare hands. But it's even more than that, for when our ancestors started messing around with stone tools all sorts of things were set in motion. Now we had to keep track of where we could find rocks in addition to water and game; we had to teach our young all of the tips and tricks of flintknapping (making stone tools); we had to carry tools with us around the parched and dangerous African landscape. All of those things helped us to keep getting smarter and smarter until we could destroy ourselves and the environment at the same time.

The big debate among paleoanthropologists is who was making these first tools.   At some point, Lucy and her friends died off (we know this for a fact because we found their bones). Later, at around 2.5 million years ago, there were actually several different forms of early humans running around in parts of east and south Africa. One of these was really big—big bones, big teeth, lots of muscle—but had a relatively small brain. He went by various names, such as Paranthropus robustus, Zinjanthropus boisei, Australopithecus robustus, and Sylvesterus stallonensis, but because he had difficulty pronouncing any of these (I'm not even going to try to tell you how to pronounce them), he often preferred to be called the Robust One.

Robust One had a couple of cousins. One was much smaller in virtually every way, and was called Australopithecus africanus, or the Gracile One. And finally, there is our hero, Homo habilis. In most ways Homo habilis looked more or less like the Gracile One, but had a slightly larger brain.

So, which one made the tools?   Professor Philip Tobias, the scientist who named him, believed that habilis was the one responsible, and concluded this largely on the basis of his big head (habilis' big head, not Tobias's). But other scholars have pointed out that stone tools have been found at sites with none of the three forms – Robust, Gracile, or habilis—present, or sometimes with Robust ones only, or sometimes with two or three of the forms together. So, it isn't true that habilis is always around when stone tools are found. In fact, if we do a statistical study to see who is most often found with stone tools (and therefore most likely to have been the real tool-maker), it turns out that we'd have to conclude that antelope were making the tools! Also, studies of the hand bones suggest that any of the three forms were physically capable of making the tools.

Unfortunately, the evidence really isn't there yet to allow us to say conclusively which form made the tools, and so some scientists are waiting until we find a skeleton with a tool actually in one of the hands. Of course, this would still leave open the possibility that the skeleton belonged to an individual who was murdered by one of the rival forms, and the stone stool then placed in his hand only to make it look like a suicide! This shows how difficult it is to get any concrete answers in prehistory.

One of the earliest stone tool cultures is called the Oldowan ('Old' meaning 'old' and 'owan' meaning 'very'), which also relates to the fact that it is well represented at the site of Olduvai ('uvai' is another variant of 'very') Gorge. This is, of course, a very famous Kenyan site that was excavated by Drs. Louis and Mary Leakey. The Leakey family represents one of the great names in paleoanthropological history due to the number of great discoveries they made. As one colleague of mine noted recently, though, none of their theories holds much water.

Going over all those names of early hominids (and believe me, there are more than that out there in the scientific literature) brings me back one of the points I was trying to make in the last chapter, namely names. Remember how I told you that there were certain rules about naming fossils? Well, one of them that I didn't tell you about is this: anytime you find a new fossil, be sure to give it a new name regardless of how much it may look to anyone else like some other

19

previously found fossil. This is called the "Splitter's Creed," which is in stark contrast to "Lumper's Law."

You see, there are two kinds of paleoanthropologists: splitters and lumpers. Splitters like to give new names to every newly found fossil; lumpers recognize that many fossils that were originally given different names are actually the same species and should therefore have the same name.   These two teams compete with each other all the time.

Here's how the game works.   First, the splitters go out and find several dozen scraps of fossil bone, most of them microscopic in size. Each scrap of bone is given a new name (keeping the various donors happy) and, magically almost, one of those scraps always appears to be the new "missing link" between apes and humans. This, of course, brings lots of attention to the split- ter, because people have been looking for that particular link since the time of Darwin. (Actually, to digress a bit, it is impossible to have the missing link in your possession. After all, once it is found it won't be missing any more.)

Anyway, after allowing the splitter some time in the spotlight, the intrepid lumper goes forth and declares that half of the scraps found by the splitter actually represent the same species (sometimes even the same individual), and the other half are just pieces of fossilized chickens. Ergo (Latin for "ha, ha"), the new finds should all be given the same name, and more important, they should be given the name of the first-recognized member of that species (who was, most often, found by the lumper's uncle). This makes the splitter very angry and for a couple of years there are nasty exchanges as hundreds of acres of prime forest are turned to paper on which numerous articles and books are written, published, and then forgotten.

Then the whole thing starts over again.

Well, we're not going to know who really made the tools for some time, and we're cer- tainly not going to stop the splitter/lumper debates. But that shouldn't prevent us from enjoy- ing a good meal. Chef Dan thought that Oldowan Omelets might be just the thing, which can be especially good if they are made from ostrich eggs like in the old days. If that doesn't suit your taste, you might want to try the Habilis Hash.

Study Questions

1. How long do you think it took for early hominids to realize that it was easier to break one rock against another instead of against their heads?

2. Which would you rather be and why: a splitter, a lumper, or a professional hockey player?

3. Would the world be better or worse without Paleolithic archaeology? No, wait—don't answer that—I'll rephrase it. How about, Where would we be today if the die of human evolution had not been forged by the fork in the path represented by the anecdote of lithic technology? Explain what this question is trying to ask.

Oldowan Omelet

1 tbs. butter
1 big ostrich egg or 3 large chicken eggs
2 oz. cream cheese cut in small cubes
2 oz. smoked salmon, cut into small pieces
salt and pepper to taste
caviar

Scramble the eggs together. Salt and pepper if desired. Heat an omelet pan with the butter. I recommend a non-stick 7" pan for this. Pour the eggs in when the pan is good and hot. Work the cooked eggs towards the middle so the uncooked eggs move to the bottom of the pan. If you feel comfortable doing it, you can try flipping the omelet in the pan (practice this first before showing off to your friends!). Place the cream cheese and salmon on top and warm in the oven for just a moment. Slide the omelet onto a plate folding it over with the pan as it comes out. Place a small dollop of caviar on top of the omelet and serve with your favorite breakfast accompaniments.

Habilis Hash

2 lbs. leftover roast or corned beef, cooked medium-well
5–6 medium-sized potatoes, peeled and shredded
1 small onion, shredded
1 cup beef stock or broth
1 stick melted butter

     Dig out that leftover roast or corned beef from the refrigerator and dice it into very small pieces, or even better, shred it. Combine the diced meat and the potatoes in a mixing bowl. Grate the onion into the mixture. Mix 2 tablespoons of the butter and just enough of the stock to make the mixture moist but not wet. Heat some of the butter in a pan and form the mixture into patties. Fry in the pan until golden brown on both sides. Enjoy with your favorite-style eggs.

Man the Hunter, or Man the Scavenger?

It's fairly clear that at about 2.5 million years ago our ancestors were eating meat. We know this because most of the sites of this period are littered with various animal bones and some of these actually show cutmarks made by early stone tools. These sites, with all of this rotting bone and flesh strewn about, must have reeked at the time. This may be why humans lost a keen sense of smell. But let's not get into that now—this is a cookbook and the whole idea is to whet the appetite, not destroy it.

One of the debates—and I don't want to give the impression that paleoanthropologists argue about everything, but rather I would like to state explicitly that this is the case—has to do with how these hominids got their meat.

Some of us might remember that in the days before McDonald's and Burger King, the only way to get a good, juicy steak was to go out and hunt it yourself. So, if the Australopithecines and/or Homo habilis were eating meat, they must have been hunting, right? Well, not necessarily.

Remember, on the African plain there is another way to get meat and that's by scavenging. As disgusting and, well, unmanly as this may sound, this is not that stupid an idea: instead of approaching a mad hippo or wildebeest armed only with a broken rock (OK, you're the one with the rock, not the hippo, but still …), wouldn't it be easier just to munch on the leftovers of some lion kill?   We all know that these African predators are real killing machines. Instead of competing directly with them, why not let them do the dirty work and afterwards just enjoy the fruits of their labor?   This, then, marks the real beginnings of the concept of middle management, which is one of the fundamental traits of modern humans.

But this doesn't mean that life was all gravy, and actually scavenging for food raised a lot of issues. First of all, how do you tell a lion to move over and let you have a turn at the carcass? This question prompted some archaeologists to do experiments with living lions to see how cooperative they (the lions) would be. They (the archaeologists) were able to conclude, just seconds before they became meals themselves, that just trying to snatch food away from a hungry carnivore is not always very effective.

Archaeologists often try various kinds of experiments in the hopes of seeing for themselves what life in the prehistoric past was like. For want of a better term, this is called " experimental archaeology." The simple fact is, we don't always know how the tools and such that we find in the ground were actually used in the past. Unlike ethnographers, who can simply ask their informants to explain or demonstrate, we pretty much have to figure things out for ourselves. This can be challenging at times, and also pretty funny. The bottom line, though, is that archaeologists can experience for themselves the true meaning of "survival of the fittest," and it means that there are usually plenty of job openings for our younger colleagues.

So let's say that hominids waited until the lions or hyenas or whatever were finished with their meal before moving in and picking on what was left over. This seems to be the more likely way of doing it, though our furry friends still had to be on guard against the carnivores coming back for seconds, or worse yet, for dessert. So it was still a dangerous life, but hey—it definitely beat scrounging around for seeds and tubers.

The other problem these early "hunters" faced was that they lived before the invention of matches, lighters, or electric starters, which meant that they probably ate most of their meat raw. So, if it isn't disgusting enough to imagine eating scavenged carcasses, imagine eating them cold, dried-out, stringy, and dirty. It's clear, however, that such a life provided a major reason to hurry up the evolutionary process.

What all this means is that the old notion of "Man the Hunter," as something deep within our genes, is probably wrong. "Man the Lazy Bum" is probably more accurate, which explains why men today would rather scavenge a bag of cheese doodles while watching Sunday football than take the time to kill their own food.

Which brings up another question: Why do some people insist that the human body is better suited for a life of vegetarianism than of carnivory? One of the interesting things learned by observing other primates in the wild is that even creatures as cuddly and furry as chimps will kill smaller animals—tearing them apart with their bare hands—and devour them. Furthermore, no one has ever observed chimps in the wild eating tofu or a large mixed salad with dressing on the side. Even vegetarian lasagna is completely unknown in the wild. So, don't feel guilty about pulling over and taking that road kill back to the family for a nice feast—it's what being human is all about.

With a little hard work (something he's not really accustomed to), Chef Dan has come up with a hearty recipe that recreates those long-lost days on the African plain. We guarantee that after a couple of good helpings of his Serengeti Scavenger Stew you'll be ready to face down any predator, either at home or in the office.

27

Serengeti Scavenged Stew

4 lb. meat (scavenged is best but make sure the road kill is fresh so as
        to avoid too much bacteria growth)
2 oz. vegetable oil
2 medium-sized onions
4 cloves garlic (or even more if you like it as much as I do)
4–6 tbs. flour
2 cups red wine
4 cups beef broth
4 carrots
4 stalks of celery
20 red-skin potatoes (smaller than a baseball but larger than a golfball)
1 cup tomato concasse (which means coarsely chopped)

Cut the meat into bite-sized cubes. I like pieces about 1- 1/2-inch, but any size
you like is good. Heat a soup pot until it is hot. I like a good heavy pot like a cast iron
but any good stockpot will do. Put the oil into the hot pan and brown the meat in it.
After the meat is browned, add the carrots, celery, and onions. Cook these together
until the onions become translucent. Add the garlic and sauté for about thirty seconds.
Then add flour and stir until incorporated. Add the tomato concasse and then the red
wine. Cook the wine for a couple of minutes and then add the beef stock. I like to
make my own stock, but this being a family book I won't put the kids to sleep with the
procedure. A good broth from the store will do.

(continued on next page)

Now here comes the fun part. Use herbs. If you have lamb, use rosemary, thyme, bay leaf, salt, pepper to taste. I don't measure these. Use your taste. It will tell you what is good. If you have beef, use thyme, bay leaf, basil, or anything you like. Experiment! This is what makes it good. Try tarragon, oregano, chervil, or marjoram. If you use game meat like venison, squirrel, rabbit, and the like, then the stronger herbs like rosemary are best. Simmer this for about an hour, adding stock as needed. After an hour add the potatoes and cook for about twenty minutes more or until they are tender. Adjust the seasoning and serve. I like a nice crusty French bread with mine. This should serve 8–10 people.

Study Questions

1. Speaking of road kills, is it a coincidence that fast-food hamburger restaurants started after the invention of the automobile?
2. Which would you rather do and why: face down an angry hippo or chase away a pride of lions from their dinner? And what do you call a bunch of hippos, anyway – a hoard, herd, gaggle, school, or flock?
3. Before the invention of football, what did men to do to waste time?

World Colonists, or Out of Africa (Part 1)

There is little doubt that the earliest humans arose in Africa, but by about 1.5 million years ago they started getting restless and decided to move on. Over the next few hundred thousand years they eventually colonized most of the Old World, including the Middle East, Europe, and South and East Asia. You shouldn't get the impression that they were too restless, however, since they moved at an average rate of about 75 feet per year, or between 2 and 3 inches per day. Many people think that the entire move was accomplished simply by rolling over in their sleep night after night.

What kind of people were these daring, though incredibly slow, travelers? Generally they go by the scientific name of Homo erectus, but some splitters like to also recognize a form called Homo ergaster. They were probably a bit smarter than their earlier Australopithecine ancestors, though their brains were still not as large as ours. You might say that they were a bit slow in both senses of the term.

Homo erectus is often identified by the kind of stone tools that were made, what are called handaxes or bifaces. Generally they are rather large tools, roughly triangular or oval in shape, with flakes removed from two opposite sides. Believe it or not, nobody has a clue what they were used for—the only thing we do agree on is that they probably were not really used as axes. More likely they were a kind of all-purpose butchering tool.

One real innovation, and one that was at the heart of their successful adaptation and—more importantly—gets to the heart of this book, was the "invention" of fire. This allowed them to develop a whole new way of eating. Unfortunately, the invention of cooking utensils came somewhat later.

The name given to the culture of Homo erectus or Homo ergaster—the handaxes, plus a few other kinds of stone tools made on flakes—is called the Acheulian (pronounced a-SHOO-lee-an, and often followed by someone else saying "ge-ZOONT-hite"). The Acheulian lasts a long, long time—about 1.5 million years, which, again, is probably a reflection of the slowness of Homo erectus. A few of Chef Dan's Biface Blinis probably hit the spot after a rough day's crawl.

On his way to other parts of the world, Homo erectus acted pretty much like any other tourist—travel a bit, stop for a picnic now and then (of course leaving his trash along the way), visit local sights (or "sites," as we archaeologists like to say), and generally have a good time. Well, maybe not that good a time: it seems that we find a lot of skulls of Homo erectus here and there. This has led some paleoanthropologists to speculate that most, if not all, of these early pioneers eventually died.

What are some of the sites where Homo erectus stayed on his way around the Old World? One of the early places he visited, located just off the African continent in sunny Israel, is Ubeidiya (oo-be-DEE-ya). The main attraction to this site, besides the fact that it's not far from the beaches of the Mediterranean, is that it is tilted. Yes, that's right, the whole site is turned on its side, which means that archaeologists get to excavate it standing up. While this is good for the archaeologist, it would seem to be an uncomfortable place for Homo erectus to stay (how did he sleep at night without rolling down to the center of the earth?). It does show, however, how adaptable good ol' erectus (or ergaster) was. Either that, or the hauntingly good taste of Chef Dan's Ubeidiya Jambalaya made it all worthwhile.

Another fun spot, just at the gates of Europe, is the Georgian site of Dmanisi (pronounced de-min-EE-see), which, at about 1.7 million years (or some argue that it is 800,000 years old) (ok, what's 900,000 years of uncertainty—it's not like our discipline lacks precision or any-

Early BBQ

thing), is currently the oldest site outside of Africa.   This of course made everyone connected with the site very famous, and so today there are more archaeologists per square foot at Dmanisi than at just about any other Paleolithic site in the world. This often happens since archaeologists compete for media attention just like everyone else.   Chef Dan's Dmanisi Dumplings have been developed to feed a whole gaggle (or school or flock or bunch) of hungry archaeologists competing with one another for the spotlight.

Making his or her way across Europe, our distant relatives eventually made it to Spain, and a whole group of them decided to stay several hundreds of thousands of years at a site call Atapuerca (ah-tuh-PWEAR-ka)—when I say a whole group, I mean just that: several individuals of all ages were found there. The excavators of this site believe that they represent some ancient sacrifice, although others believe that a group of these Homo antecessor (oops—more splitting going on) accidentally fell into the cave through an opening in the top, or that they are just the remains of some kind of meal. Anyway you look at it, it's hard to conclude that life was much fun in those days!

34

Of course, what trip to Europe would be complete without a stop in Jolly Olde England? Homo erectus/ergaster/antecessor thought the same way we do and he somehow managed to leave several of his body parts and Acheulian (gesundheit!) tools scattered about the country. One of the most spectacular of these is a site called Boxgrove (BOX-grove—one of the five or six English names that is actually pronounced like it is spelled), which is located right on the beach. Although the excavations there have so far failed to turn up the normal beach equipment (volleyballs, frisbees, etc), there is little doubt that some Boxgrove Beach Barbeque would have been a big hit with these English erecti (or ergasteri or antecessori or whateveri).

The final stop for our jet-setting heros (well, ok, maybe jet-setting isn't the right word when talking about people who moved 2–3 inches a day) is at a site called Zhoukoudian (zyo-ko-TYEN), located not far from the modern city of Beijing, China.   Back in the 1930s when this site

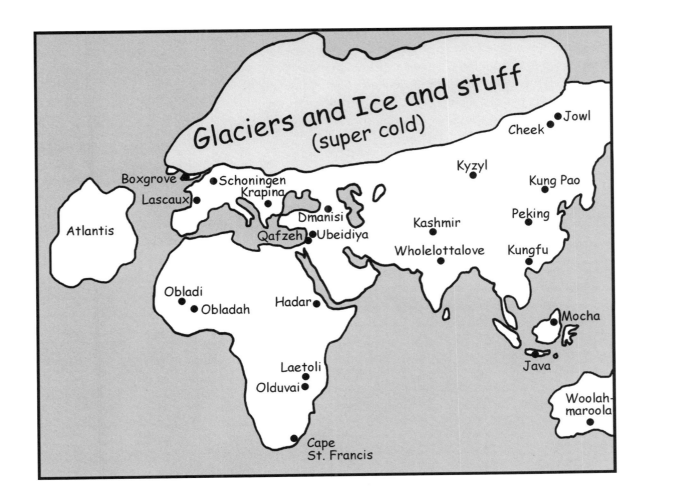

was first excavated, Beijing was known as Peking, and Zhoukoudian was called Choukoutien, and the fossils were called Homo voyeurensis, or "Peeking Man." Unfortunately, all of the original fossils from Zhoukoudian were lost or stolen at the beginning of World War II as they were being shipped to the United States. Paleoanthropologists have been keeping their eyes out for the original Peking Man ever since. To commemorate this spectacular find, and the less-than-spectacular loss, Chef Dan couldn't resist presenting you with his own version of Beijing Duck.

Study Questions

1. Doesn't the name Homo erectus sound a bit silly? What name would you give to a creature with a brain only three-quarters of the size of ours (how about Homo congress manensis)?

2. If bifaces were two-faced, does that make Homo erectus a hypocrite? And what do you think of the term hippocrite to describe a bunch of hippos? Explain.

36

Biface Blinis

2-1/2 cups scalded milk
1 package yeast (about one tablespoon)
2 tsp. sugar
3 cups flour
3 eggs, separated
4 tbs. melted butter
1/2 tsp. salt
1/4 cup sour cream

Scald the milk and cool until warm. Put the yeast in the warm milk and add the sugar. Let stand for 5 minutes. In an electric mixer combine all the ingredients except the egg whites. Mix well. Let stand for about 30 minutes until the mixture doubles in size.

In the meantime whip the egg whites in a separate bowl. Fold them into the batter. Allow to stand for 10 minutes while you heat a non-stick pan. Lightly butter and spoon the batter into the pan so they are 3–4 inches in diameter. Fry until golden and flip. When they are golden on both faces (hence "bifacial") remove them and keep warm under a damp cloth.

Traditionally these are served warm with sour cream and caviar, which I recommend you try. You might also try them with ricotta cheese sweetened with a bit of sugar and some fresh fruit—whatever kind of fruit you can gather will do. Even try them with your favorite jelly, or the gravlax that we'll make in a few hundred-thousand years (a couple of chapters later). You'll have to move more than 3 inches per day if you want to get these for yourself before they're gone.

Ubeidiya Jambalaya

There are many brands of Cajun seasoning available at the market these days and you may find it easier to pick one of these up for this, but I am going to list the seasonings I use for this dish.

2 bay leaves
1/2–1 tsp. cayenne
1 tsp. oregano
1/2 tsp. basil
1/2 tsp. thyme
1/4 tsp. white pepper
1/2 tsp. black pepper
salt to taste
2 tbs. olive oil
1/2 cup tomato sauce
1 cup peeled and diced tomatoes
2 cups chicken stock

1/2 cup diced chicken
1/2 cup Tasso (Cajun-seasoned ham)
1/2 cup chopped Andouille sausage or Polish sausage
2 medium onions chopped
2 stalks celery chopped
1 medium green bell pepper chopped
    (you may adjust the peppers to suit your taste. I get heavy with it sometimes because I like it hot)
1 bulb garlic chopped (yes the whole bulb— obviously not the best choice for a first date)
2 cups uncooked converted rice

(continued on next page)

You will need to score the tomatoes and put them in boiling water for about 30 seconds. Then, immediately dunk them into ice water to stop the cooking. This should loosen the skin so they peel easily. After peeling the skin, cut in half and gently squeeze most of the seeds out. Then, dice up the flesh and set aside.

Heat the oil in a heavy stockpot. A cast-iron Dutch oven works great here. Add the ham and sausage and sauté about 5 minutes until crisp. Add the onions, celery, and bell pepper and sauté until the onions are translucent. Add the chicken, garlic, diced tomatoes, and seasoning and cook about 1–2 minutes, being careful not to burn the garlic. Add the tomato sauce and cook 2 minutes. Add the stock and rice and stir well. Cover the pot and place in a 350-degree oven until the rice is tender, about 30–40 minutes. Serve immediately. Don't forget the crispy French bread called baguette.

Boxgrove Beach Barbeque

This one should be made a day ahead of time so the flavors develop. "Flavor?" you say. "How can there be any flavor if this is an English dish?" Look, let's not start an international incident here—just try it.

This can be made with leftover beef or pork roasts, but the best way is to get a nice pork shoulder from the butcher and smoke it slowly until it is tender and pulls apart from the bone. If you do not have a smoker, you may roast the meat in a 300-degree oven until its internal temperature reaches 150 degrees. Cool the roast and cut into cubes or pull it from the smoked bone. Place this into a saucepot and cover with your favorite barbecue sauce. There are plenty of good ones on the market these days or you may make your own. Add a couple of cups of chicken stock to this and bring to a boil on the stove. When it comes to a boil, turn it down and simmer it for 2 hours, stirring frequently. You may need to add more stock as it cooks and thickens. Cool down and store in the refrigerator overnight.

To serve, first scrape off the excess fat that will rise the top while it is cooling. Then heat to a boil and serve on a nice Kaiser roll. I like it with slaw on it too, or on the side as you like.

Dmanisi Dumplings

1 lb. flour
8 fluid oz. hot water
1 lb. ground pork (raw)
4 cloves garlic
4 minced water chestnuts
1 tsp. minced ginger
3 tbs. soy sauce

1/4 cup shredded cabbage
2 onions, diced
1 egg whites
2 tsp. sesame oil
1 tsp. sugar
salt and pepper to taste
chicken stock

Mix the flour and water together and set aside for about thirty minutes. Meanwhile, combine the remaining ingredients except the broth and test it by cooking a small piece. Adjust seasonings if necessary. Divide the dough into small balls of about 1–2 oz. Roll out with a rolling pin into circles. Place a small amount of the meat mixture into the center of the dumpling and wrap the dough around it. Seal the dumpling tight and set aside. Stuff all the dough you have.

Bring the chicken stock to a boil and drop the dumplings into it to cook for about 10 minutes. Remove and serve with soy or your favorite dipping sauce.

I like to heat about a cup of soy sauce with a teaspoon each of chopped ginger and garlic. Add a bit of white wine and about a cup of brown sugar. Heat to dissolve the sugar. Add a pinch of red pepper flakes. Remove from heat and cool. Add one chopped green onion and serve with the dumplings. If you like it thick, mix some corn starch with cold water and add a little at a time, bringing it back to a boil each time, until it is thick enough.

Beijing Duck

4–5 lb. duck
boiling water—enough to submerge the duck
1 tsp. orange zest
1 tsp. lemon zest
2 tbs. sugar
1/2 tsp. salt
1 tsp. Chinese 5 spice
1/2 cup molasses
1/2 cup honey
1/4 cup hot water
4 tbs. rice wine vinegar
Beijing pancakes—recipe following
hoisan sauce—you can find this in most grocery stores

    Blanch the duck in the boiling water for 5 minutes. Remove and place on a draining rack for 15 minutes. Rub the orange and lemon zest, sugar, salt, and Chinese 5 spice in the cavity of the duck. Sew the openings closed, or you can use poultry pins.

    Combine the molasses, honey, hot water, and vinegar and slowly pour over the outside of the duck. Pour a little at a time and let drain off until mixture is gone. This may take 10 minutes or so. Allow the duck to dry for 3–4 hours (using a fan will help this process along).

    Place the duck in a 400-degree oven on a roasting rack for 10 minutes and then turn the oven down to 350. Roast the duck for 25 minutes per pound. Slice the duck into thin strips and place on the Beijing pancakes with some hoisan sauce. Roll these up and serve. Garnish with some green onions cut into brushes or sliced.

Beijing Pancakes

3 cups flour
1-1/4 cups boiling water
2 tbs. sesame oil

Add the boiling water to the flour and mix into dough. Add the sesame oil and knead together. Add a bit more water if they are too dry. Let stand for 20 minutes. Roll the dough into pancakes and cook in a non-stick pan until light brown on both sides. You can do these ahead of time and warm in the oven with a damp towel over them.

Hey Kids !

Cut out along the dotted lines and dress up Thag in modern clothes !

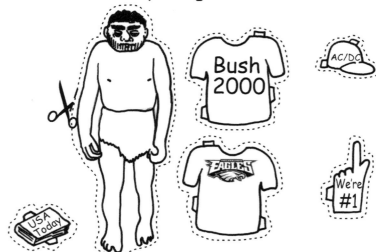

See how hard it would be to spot a neanderthal if he walked past you on the street ? Wouldn't be easy, huh?

Neanderthals

Things get really exciting in human evolution when we get to the point where Neanderthals roamed the earth. For one thing, most people think of Neanderthals as the quintessential "Cavemen." So, if you are going to make a movie about human evolution, you're going to include Neanderthals. You might be tempted to throw in a few dinosaurs, but that would be wrong. Most dinosaurs died out about 80 million years ago and the rest evolved into chickens. Neanderthals didn't appear until about 200,000 years ago or so. So while they almost lived at the same time, dinosaurs and Neanderthals just missed each other by about 79.8 million years. But hey, if it makes the movie more successful, do it.

Actually, this brings us to one of the biggest problems in paleoanthropology, namely that nobody has been able to produce a truly successful movie on cavepersons. Even though the subject is interesting to a lot of people, and even though it can include all sorts of sex and violence, the simple fact is that caveperson movies don't do reel well .

I happen to have a theory as to why this is so. It is because everyone seems to have strong opinions on what Neanderthals were like, but there is no real consensus. Some people think Neanderthals were stupid (as in the classic insult "You are a Neanderthal, moron!") and others think that they were smart (as in the equally classic, "Wow—that's fantastic. You must be some sort of Neanderthal Einstein!"). In other words, some people think they were stoop-shouldered, sloped-foreheaded, bent-at-the-knees, incredibly hairy, grunting idiots, and others think that they are just like anyone else from, say, Philadelphia. Wait—that's saying the same thing! (Just kidding, friends and neighbors in Philly).

Anyway, when a movie about Neanderthals comes out, its portrayal of them is certain to run counter to half the population's preconceived view of Neanderthals, and those people are going to criticize the movie as being inaccurate.   Yeah, right—like Star Wars Episode I is accurate!   And see, this really is my point.   Films like Star Wars and Star Trek pretty much defined how space movies are supposed to be.   When we go to one of those movies we don't thumb through back issues of "Modern Rocket Scientist" to verify that all the facts are right.   We don't care about the facts, so long as it looks "right."   So, for example, we love to watch fighter space jets bank through a tight turn, forgetting the simple fact that in space there is no air against which you can bank.   Likewise, we all know what a laser gun sounds like—tzeeew-tzeeeew—and if we heard one go click-click, well, we'd know that that was just a fake.   So, if we're able to accept a bit of inaccuracy in space movies just for the sake of entertainment, why can't we do the same for Neanderthals?

My favorite caveman movie, by the way, is "Clan of the Cave Bear" because I made the stone tools that were used in it.   And while like every other caveperson movie it was criticized as being inaccurate and so forth, I like to point out that not one person has criticized the stone tools. I do feel cheated, however, that I was not nominated for an Academy Award in the category of "Best Period Props in an Early Hominid Drama."

Anyway, somehow we got off the subject of what the Neanderthals were really like.   In many ways they were a lot like us—us being what we call modern Homo sapiens.   They were not bent-kneed, and they had brains as large as our own.   But they did have big brow ridges, they were extremely muscular, and they didn't have much of a chin.   Go beyond that, however, and nobody, not even the paleoanthropologists, can agree.   In fact, the whole subject of Neanderthals—everything from their behavior to their place in human evolution—is the most hotly debated in all of paleoanthropology.

Never watch a caveman movie with an anthropologist

Were they the same species as us (Homo sapiens), or were they a different species (Homo neanderthalensis)? Nobody knows. Could they, or did they talk? Nobody agrees. Did they have religion or bury their dead? Some people say yes, and others say no. Is their name spelled Neandertal or Neanderthal? Not many agree. So, is there a reason why the public is so confused on this issue? Yes, because even we so-called experts are confused. What this means is that there will not be a good Caveperson movie for quite a few years.

We'll go over some of these issues in the following chapters, but before we do, you might want to take a break and get some energy. Try making a batch of Chef Dan's Neanderthal Nibblers. Then you'll be ready to face the challenge of coming face-to-face with the Neanderthals.

48

Study Questions

1. Is it just a coincidence that the letters in Neandertal also spell out Rental Dean?

2. Discuss why it would have been much better if Crichton had called his book "Pleistocene Park" and unleashed a bevy (or gaggle or bunch) of reconstituted Neanderthals on a small Midwestern town, who hacked to pieces the mayor and several shopkeepers with stone weapons before eventually the townspeople brought in a strong, silent, and extremely handsome Paleolithic archaeologist from a large Eastern University (maybe one located in Philadelphia) who, by using a quickly assembled repertoire of guteral gestures (whatever those are), was able to calm down the Neanderthals, who became model members of the community and helped fight the school of Tyranosaurus rex (or maybe "rexes" or "rexi"?) that were unleased in the sequel.

Neanderthal Nibblers

5 lbs. pork back ribs (peeled—ask your butcher to do this for you)
your favorite barbecue sauce (I like sweet sauce)
2 tbs. pickling spice
2 dashes Worcestershire sauce
1/4 cup white wine
enough water to cover the ribs

Combine the water, pickling spice, Worcestershire sauce, and wine in a pot and bring to a boil. Cook the ribs in the water for one hour or until the meat just starts to pull off the bones. Remove them and cool. Brush on the barbecue sauce and broil for 1–2 minutes, just until the sauce cooks on. Be careful not to burn the barbecue. Remove and brush on more barbecue. Place back under the broiler. Repeat this process four times. Remove the ribs and cut them into pieces of one or two bones each. Just big enough to be appetizer size.

Reheat in the oven just until hot. Enjoy.

Hint: Leave the ribs whole or cut in half and you have a great rib dinner. All you need is some mashed taters and cole slaw.

The Middle Paleolithic or Mousterian

The Mousterian (moose-STEER-ee-un) is the name given to the stone tool complex that is most commonly associated with Neanderthals. In many ways it is not that different from the Acheulian that preceded it. Let's take a closer look at some of these tools.

Most of the tools characteristic of the Mousterian are made on flakes (remember? the sharp bits of stone that come off when you hit one rock with another). These flake tools come in a wide variety of shapes and sizes, and for a long time people didn't know what to call them or how to interpret them. But thanks to a French prehistorian, François Bordes, we now have a complete typology that allows us to count up how many of this type or that type we find when digging a Mousterian site.

One of the more common types we find is called a scraper. This is a tool that has one or two or even three edges worked to be smooth and sharp. We don't really know what they were used for, however. Some people think they were used for scraping hides, others think they were for whittling wood, and others argue that they were knives. Probably they were used for a little bit of everything—kind of the original Swiss Army Knives.

Then there are the notches and denticulates. A notch is just what it sounds like—a flake with a bit of a concavity made on one of the edges. A denticulate is a flake with several notches together, producing a kind of toothed or serrated edge. Again, we don't really know what they were used for. Some people think they were used for scraping hides; others think they were for whittling wood; and others argue that they were knives. Probably they were used for a little bit of everything—kind of the original Swiss Army Knives.

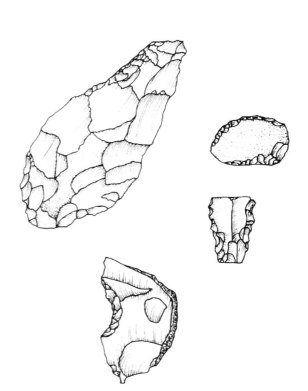

Am I being redundant? Or maybe I'm just saying the same thing twice. In either case, we don't know much about what these things were used for, or what Neanderthals did with them. We don't know their functions. We don't even know what purpose they served. In case you didn't notice, I think I've set a new record in this paragraph: redundancy times two, or redundancy squared. In my years of teaching I've found that a little repetition doesn't hurt, and that sometimes repeating myself can be good: it's a great way of stretching out 30 minutes of lecture into a full hour.

To get back to the point, finally, there are also bifaces in the Mousterian, and just as is the case with the bifaces in the Acheulian (gesundheit!), we don't really know what they were used for either. Some people think they were used for scraping hides, others think—oh, forget it. You know what I'm going to say by now.

I find that students just love to learn all about these different kinds of stone tools. When you come right down to it, archaeology is one of those fields for which you get to learn all sorts of interesting tidbits about people who are long dead and who basically have no relevance to our own time.   Spending your time learning all 63 stone tool types from the Mousterian (that's right, François Bordes defined 63 different types!) is much more fascinating that having to learn how to read actuarial tables (whatever they are) or how to build new kinds of bio-weapons, or anything else you might think is more "current." When students are first confronted with this new knowledge in one of my classes, the conversation usually goes something like this:

Student #1: Do we have to learn all of the 63 types for the exam?

Me: Of course.

Student #2: Wait a minute—is this relevant to anything in our lives?

Me: Absolutely—it's relevant to the grade you'll get in this course.

Student #1: I'm dropping the course.

Now, I'm not trying to make it sound like all students are whining, spoiled little brats who are here (at their parents' expense) only to learn what will make them (the students—obviously there's no payback for the parents) money: they are also interested in parties. So I quickly point out to them that naming all 63 types is the perfect party game and that members of the opposite sex are actually fascinated by someone who can speak intelligently about the differences between scrapers and denticulates.   I don't know how many times, for example, I've heard the following exchange take place during an undergraduate social event:

53

Student #1: Hey, I really like that smile of yours and the fact that you're missing
several teeth—it reminds me of those beautiful Mousterian denticulates. Would you
care to come back to my dorm room and take a look at some lithic types?

Student #2: Get lost, geek.

Anyway, to return to the subject at hand, what you find when you dig through a Mousterian site, then, is a variety of scrapers, notches, denticulates, and maybe some handaxes. Some sites have more scrapers, some have more denticulates, and so forth. Then we archaeologists spend several years arguing about what that means. Chef Dan has come up with his own interpretation: the Mousterian hors d'oeuvres tray, with a sampling of a little bit of everything, including some Cinnamon Scrapers, Flint Fritters, and Hand Axe Peppers. You can follow this up

NEANDERTHAL CAVES
MAGAZINE
THIS ISSUE
CAVE OF THAG
CAVE TOO CLEAN? READ 10 TIPS TO FILTHY LIVING

with some tasty Mousterian Goulash. Try this out the next time you have a dinner party for a group of Swiss soldiers—they will love it and feel right at home.

Speaking of food, what are the real facts about Neanderthal nutrition? Recent studies by some of my colleagues at the University of Pennsylvania have shown that Neanderthals were really very healthy people. This is because they knew how to eat well-balanced meals full of good, wholesome, and natural ingredients. Of course, there are some controversies about their diet and even how they acquired their food.

In truth, Neanderthals must have been fairly disgusting people. When you excavate a Neanderthal site what you find is a jumble of stone tools, the debris left over from making those tools, and lots of bones representing the remains of their meals. In other words, they were living right on top of their own trash. Can you imagine living like this? It would be like living on top of a garbage dump, or perhaps certain parts of New Jersey.

What kinds of bones do we find? Depending on where and when they lived we see lots of large game, such as buffalo, wild cattle, horse, deer, and reindeer.   Small animals are less common, and fish and birds are rare. Unfortunately, we don't have much idea of what they may have eaten in the way of vegetables—broccoli, asparagus, and most members of the lettuce family do not preserve well.

At a few Mousterian sites we have been lucky enough to find some long, sharpened wooden implements. Many people have interpreted these as spears, and in a couple of cases, especially at the site of Schoningen in Germany, such implements have been found in association with horses. This raises the interesting possibility that maybe in those days horses were big-game hunters themselves. On the other hand, Professor Clive Gamble has suggested that these may not be spears at all, but were instead used by Neanderthals to probe beneath the snow-covered landscape in search of frozen carcasses.   Our own Chef Dan has suggested an even more likely interpretation: they were Pleistocene-sized kabob skewers!   What a perfect way to serve up a few bulls and horses to the hungry troops!

There are a couple of sites where we see evidence of a really tasty treat, with the main dish being their fellow Neanderthals. At the site of Krapina (CRAP-in-a, and yes, as Dave Barry would say, I'm not making that up), for example, there are many Neanderthal bones with clear evidence of burning. At other sites, we have found Neanderthal bones with cutmarks made from stone tools, probably reflecting butchery. What we don't know is whether this represents a kind of ceremonial cannibalism, conditions of starvation, or just one more example of how Neanderthals were disgusting. At any rate, if you are what you eat, as the saying goes, then we have to conclude that the Neanderthals were just being themselves.

Chef Dan had wanted to include a recipe here for his famous Neanderthal People Parts in a light truffle sauce, but we decided finally that it might be a little too much for our gentle readers. Maybe in the second edition. In the meantime, enjoy some of his Mousterian Big Game Kabobs.

Study Questions

1. What is your favorite Mousterian tool type and why? Explain exactly how you would use it to provide food for your family. Would you expect to live for a long time like that?
2. Explain in detail why you ended up spending good money on this stupid book in the first place.
3. It's true that archaeologists learn about the past by finding and analyzing the discarded trash of our ancestors. Do you think that this reason alone is sufficient to designate the state of New Jersey as our official National Archaeological Site (state motto: "Come Dig Us")?

Mousterian Goulash

My friend from Hungary gave me this recipe and I want to pass it along to you.

2 lbs. beef chuck cut into 1–2 inch squares
2 medium onions, diced
2 tbs. vegetable oil
1/4 cup Hungarian paprika
2 bay leaves
1 quart water
4 large potatoes peeled and diced
salt and pepper to taste
sour cream

Heat the oil in a heavy saucepan. A cast-iron Dutch oven works well here, too. When it is good and hot add the onions and caramelize, which is when the onions start to turn caramel colored. Add the beef and the paprika. Turn down the heat and add half of the water. Let beef simmer on low for an hour. Add the remaining water and potatoes and cook until the potatoes are tender. Salt and pepper to taste and serve with a dollop of sour cream.

Flint Fritters

1 large egg, lightly beaten
3/4 cup whole milk
1 cup flour
1 tsp. baking powder
1 tbs. sugar
1 tsp. salt
1/8 tsp. white pepper (black pepper will taste the same, but you'll see it in the batter)
vegetable oil for frying

Combine the dry ingredients in a bowl. Add the egg and milk and mix until all the dry ingredients are wet. This should make a batter a bit thicker than pancake batter. This is a basic recipe for fritters.

(continued on next page)

58

Now comes the fun part, the flint if you will. The part you can shape to your liking. You can make all kinds of fritters. Shave the corn from two ears for corn fitters. Add broccoli and cheddar. Put in crab meat and asparagus tips. Try eggplant fritters. How about blue cheese and smoked salmon or gravlax? You can add other flavoring ingredients like fresh herbs if you like.   Add another tablespoon or two of sugar and throw in your favorite fruit. Add some cinnamon and peeled apples for a delicious apple fritter. Go wild and have fun. putting as much stuff as you like in the fritter, but keep in mind that if you overload the batter it will not hold together as well.

Put enough oil in a saucepan to cover the fritter and heat it to 350 degrees. If you have a fryer then that is even better. Drop your fritters into the hot oil by the tablespoon and fry until they are golden colored. Remove with a slotted spoon and put on a plate with a paper towel to absorb excess oil. Sprinkle the fruit fritters with a bit of powdered sugar and serve immediately.

Cinnamon Scrapers

1 lb. butter
1 cup sugar
4 cups all-purpose flour
1-1/2 tsp. cinnamon

Preheat oven to 300 degrees. Cream the butter and sugar together. Combine the flour and cinnamon into a bowl. Gradually add to the butter and sugar mixture until blended, being careful not to overwork. Turn it onto a lightly floured board and pat or roll into a sheet approximately 1/2 in. thick. Refrigerate until cold. Cut into desired shapes. We prefer scraper shapes. Bake on a baking sheet for 20–30 minutes until the scrapers are sand colored. These are good with coffee or tea. And, of course, milk.

Hand Axe Peppers

12 whole chili peppers
16 oz. cream cheese
2 shallots, chopped fine
dash lemon
dash Tabasco
salt and pepper to taste
2 eggs
1 cup flour
2 cups bread crumbs
oil for frying

61

Mix the cheese, shallots, lemon, tabasco, and salt and pepper in a bowl and set aside. Cut the top off the peppers and take out the seeds. Stuff the peppers with the cheese mixture. I use a pastry bag for this but a spoon will do. Then set up three bowls. One with the beaten eggs, another with the flour, and the third with the bread crumbs. Dredge the peppers one at a time in the flour. Then get them wet in the egg. Last put them in the bread crumbs so they have a nice coating. Meanwhile, heat the oil in a fryer or saucepan to 350 degrees. Drop the peppers in the hot oil and fry until golden. Enjoy!

Mousterian Big Game Kabobs

2 lbs. lamb (this is big game to most of us city folk, but you may substitute that buffalo you nabbed this year) cut into 1-1/2 inch cubes
1 medium red onion cut into 1-1/2 inch squares
1 red bell pepper cut into 1-1/2 inch squares
1 green bell pepper cut into 1-1/2 inch squares
10 cherry tomatoes
10 button mushrooms
20 bamboo or metal skewers
1/2 cup olive oil
1 bunch fresh rosemary
1 cup balsamic vinegar (red wine vinegar works here too)
5 peppercorns
salt and pepper to taste

Alternate the meat and vegetables on the skewer. Meat, red pepper, meat, red onion, meat, green pepper, meat, tomato. New skewer. Meat, red pepper, meat, red onion, meat, green pepper, meat, mushroom. Use all skewers or meat, whichever comes first. Combine the olive oil, vinegar, chopped fresh rosemary, and peppercorns in a container and pour over the skewers. Marinate for 2 hours. Remove the skewers from the liquid and grill on a barbecue or roast in a 425-degree oven for 10–15 minutes until desired doneness. Serve these over your favorite rice or with potatoes roasted with a bit of the fresh rosemary, olive oil, and a little fresh garlic.

Pech de l'Azé Peche Melba

This recipe is named after the site in France where we are currently working.

1-1/4 cup sugar
3/4 cup water
1/4 cup + 2 tbs. white wine (I like Chablis or Chardonnay)
1 vanilla bean
8 peaches
vanilla ice cream
2 pints raspberries

Combine 1 cup sugar, vanilla bean, water, and 1/4 cup of the wine and heat to just under a simmer. Peel and stone the peaches. Place the peach halves in the poaching liquid and cook until tender. Let cool and drain the liquid. While cooling, put the raspberries, the rest of the sugar, and remaining wine in a food processor and puree. Run the puree through a fine strainer to make a smooth sauce.

To serve, place a scoop of ice cream on a plate and surround with peach halves. Pour about 2 tbs. (more if you like) of the raspberry sauce over the ice cream and enjoy.

The Origins of Modern Humans, or Out of Africa (Part 2)

Can you believe it? The whole question of the origins of modern humans is another area that has been hotly debated for a long time. I know that I'm beginning to sound like a broken record (for you young folks out there, records are the prehistoric version of CDs) about how this and that are the subject of debates. But this is a complicated question. We have to wonder, for example, what we mean by "modern," and whether or not we look at the question in relation to biology (does so-and-so look modern?) or culture (does this dumb-looking creature at least act like a modern Homo sapiens?). But these are not the real reasons for the debate. The real reason is that archaeologists and physical anthropologists love to argue about everything and this is just one more thing they can sink their intellectual teeth into (there I go using a food metaphor again).

Let me make one point perfectly clear, however: we are not a bunch of old fuddy-duddies who spend taxpayer money sitting around and arguing about stupid things. If we were, we'd be members of Congress. The truth—and it is very easy to document—is that many of us anthropology types are relatively young.

Anyway, the question still remains ... although ... I...uh... kind of forgot what it was... Oh right, where did modern humans come from? Well, there are two main schools of thought on this question. One is called the "Multiregional Continuity" school. People in this school maintain that modern Homo sapiens (HO-mo SAPE-ee-ens, which roughly translates to "people who can't seem to stop getting themselves into trouble and who are intent on destroying all life on this planet") evolved from Neanderthals all over the Old World and at about the same time (roughly between 100,000 and 40,000 years ago). "Multiregional" refers to the fact that this evolution took place in many different continents more or less independently, and "continuity" refers to the continuity between Neanderthals and us.

The other school is called the "Out of Africa" school. "Out of" in the name refers to the belief that modern Homo sapiens left or came from a particular place and spread around the world, somehow replacing aboriginal Neanderthal or Neanderthal-like populations. "Africa" you can figure out for yourself. Another name for this school is the "Garden of Eden" school. This name has never made much sense to me. For example, why would anyone leave the Garden of Eden and move to Philadelphia?

Now, the observant reader will immediately jump up and shout, "Hey—wait a minute. Didn't we already discuss the Out of Africa idea when we were talking about Homo erectus/ergaster/antecessor?" That's right, we did. But for the dispersal of Homo erectus/ergaster/antecessor we didn't have a fancy name attached to it. This is because not many people doubt that Homo erectus/ergaster/antecessor originated in Africa and ultimately spread elsewhere. Thus, we don't need a name for that. However, the origins and spread of modern humans is hotly debated, which means you have to have a short, catchy name so that you can reduce the concept down to a multiple-choice question for students in Anthropology 001. For example, consider the following sample test question:

The notion that modern humans originated in Africa and subsequently spread through out the Old World, replacing aboriginal Neanderthal populations along the way, with Robert Redford and Meryl Streep in the starring roles, is called:
    1. The Out of Arkansas hypothesis
    2. The Multiregional Continuity school
    3. The Uniregional Incontinence idea
    4. The Out of Africa model

In grading this question, you first of all have to worry about the people who answer #1, since they obviously can't read (Africa was mentioned in the question itself, stupid) or at least know nothing about geography. The second answer is a tricky one—this one will catch those who studied a little bit but who can only remember one of the catchy names, when they see it in an answer, they automatically choose it. The people who answer #3 are a little smarter and they try to figure it out: they know that #2 isn't right—in fact, it's the opposite of that one. This leads them logically, but mistakenly, to #3. Finally, those who answer #4 are given no credit because we referred to it as a "school," not a model.

That I would not give credit for #4 may seem arbitrary, but as one of my colleagues taught me years ago, that is basically what education is all about—preparing young people for the real world. Since the world is incredibly arbitrary and unfair being the opposite would be giving our young people a seriously distorted view.

I have to confess, though, that as a professor there is nothing more enjoyable than to give a multiple choice question with no right answers. In fact, the only way to get any credit for this question would be to come up to the instructor and point out that there is no right answer given. Unfortunately, talking during an exam is punishable by an automatic F. This "catch" makes everything even more unfair, which in turn gives them an even better education. Isn't college wonderful?

I know it's fascinating for you to learn that there are two different theories concerning the origins of modern humans, but I suppose that some of you would like also to know which one is correct. To those people I would say the following: Hello???? Are you listening? If we knew which one was correct we wouldn't be arguing about it, would we? You're just going to have to learn both theories and that's all there is to it.

I will point out, however, that there is little real evidence to support either of these theories. In the first place, not one fossilized road sign has been found indicating the way out of Africa. This is important because that particular continent is surrounded by water everywhere except at the extreme northeast tip. Without road signs, most of these early travelers would have walked right into an ocean and drowned.

As for the continuity theory, it just seems inconceivable that ancient populations would stay in one place throughout several millennia—the urge to travel is strong among us, and the urge to exchange genes with others is even stronger. Besides, we probably would have evolved into different species by this time, which is definitely not the case.

At this point, let's take a short break and whip up some goodies to help us study up for the next set of questions. Chef Dan has suggested a couple of snacks that will help keep you alert through any all-nighter cram session.

Study Questions

1. If you were going to pack up and move to a different continent, would you first
   a. Make sure that you were more evolved than others in your group?
   b. Pack enough food to last several hundred thousand years (to avoid having to eat the local fare)?
   c. Find a trusted cave-sitter to manage things while you were away?
   d. Buy a whole new wardrobe so as to impress whatever natives you might encounter?
   e. None of the above.
2. Why is it that we only use the word "circumnavigate" when we refer to what Ferdinand Magellan was the first to do?

Glacial Gravlax

First thing you must do here is grab your spear, net, fishing pole, bare hands, and lightning reflexes, cash or credit card, and get yourself a salmon.

You'll want two filets with the skin left on. Mix equal parts kosher or sea salt and sugar together in a bowl. Smooth this mixture evenly over the flesh side of the fish. Just enough to cover the fish. Sprinkle some fresh ground pepper over the fish. I like to put fresh dill and lemon zest (thin strips of the outer layer of skin from the lemon) on the fish as well. You may omit the lemon if you like. Or you may choose to put another kind of fresh herb in place of the dill. I like to put a shot of my favorite alcohol (vodka, gin, or cognac add nice flavors) on as well, but this may either be omitted or enjoyed on the side.

Place the filets together; skin side out, so the flesh is touching, into a casserole dish. Cover with plastic and place a weight on top of the fish. A small cutting board with canned goods works well for this to distribute the weight evenly. Refrigerate for two days, turning the fish once half way. Rinse the fish briefly after the two days and slice into thin slices at an angle (so the slices are wider). These can be eaten on pieces of bread or toast. Even crackers. Try it on a bagel with cream cheese. Or wrapped around asparagus tips.

Asparagus tips with Gravlax

Blanch some asparagus in boiling water until tender. Immediately transfer these to an ice water bath to shock them. Then cut off the tips to about 1-1/2 inches in length. Wrap a thin slice of gravlax around them and enjoy.

Brie en croûte

This is always a crowd pleaser.

1 wheel of brie (about 2 lbs.)
2 sheets of puff pastry (located in the refrigerator section of your local grocery)
strawberry preserves or sliced almonds and honey
1 egg lightly beaten

Take a melon baller or a spoon and scoop out several small scoops on the top of the brie. Smear the preserves over the top so it fills the holes. Or place the almonds over the top and drizzle honey on them. Then place it on the first pastry sheet. Place the second sheet of pastry over the top and seal the edges with the egg tight up against the brie. Cut away the excess pastry. Brush the top with the egg and bake in a 400-degree oven until the crust is golden brown. Cool slightly and serve with your favorite crackers or my favorite, baguette.

The Definition of "Modern" Homo sapiens (Part 1)

So, what do we mean by "modern?" As I said earlier, it can be a question of biology or behavior. Are modern humans those who look like other people living today? If that were the definition, I'd have to leave out certain of my relatives. Or are they those who act like people today? Or do both things have to be in place before we consider them modern?

First, let's consider what physical characteristics are typical of people today (forgetting about my relatives for the moment). For one thing, we, or at least some of us, have big brains. Now, if you remember back a few pages, so did the Neanderthals. So, if we're not going to admit that Neanderthals are "modern," then we can't use the size of their heads as the major criterion. Besides, there are a lot of people today who have pretty small heads who are just as smart as anyone else, and there are many others with heads the size of a football field (I'm thinking of certain archaeologists here) who are barely capable of completing sentences. We also can't use bipedality, since walking on two legs goes back to the earliest hominids and even more to the point, we'd have to include penguins as modern humans.

Hmmmm. What can we use to distinguish modern humans from our more archaic ancestors? It's got to be something important … something that really screams "LOOK AT ME! I AM MODERN!" What could that be?

Give up? Oh, it's so easy—what makes modern humans modern are two major things: a chin and smaller brow ridges. "Of course," you're saying to yourself, "I've always thought that having a chin is incredibly important. And brow ridges? Heavens! Why, anyone with bumps above their eyes would be soooo primitive looking."

Now, before you go around feeling strangers' heads for bumps, I should point out that there are several other important differences as well. For example, Neanderthals have a space behind their wisdom teeth, though we don't really refer to them as "wisdom" teeth with Neanderthals. And their foreheads are not quite as vertical as ours. And the large bump of bone behind their ears is a bit smaller. And their noses were a bit broader. And … well, you get the idea—there are gobs of really important differences that all combine to make us look so much more modern. Don't you feel good now that you know what really separates us from more primitive forms?

What's interesting, though, is that these kinds of biologically modern humans first evolved more than 100,000 years ago, but they still made the same kinds of stone tools as the Neanderthals. For example, one of the most famous sites for early modern humans is Qafzeh (KAHF-zuh), which is located just north of the Sea of Galilee in modern Israel. Several individuals were found here—some more modern-looking than others—but all were found with typical Mousterian kinds of tools.

Even more interesting (I know that you are on the edge of your seat right now) is this: these early moderns were living more or less cheek to jowl with Neanderthals who are found at other nearby sites. They may even have entertained each other socially. Just imagine the sorts of Neanderthal/modern mixers that might have gone on—dinner parties, volleyball matches, the Stone Age edition of Trivial Pursuit:

Q: Mammoths are:

        (a) aliens from the planet Xircon

        (b) smarter than the average Homo erectus

        (c) extinct

        (d) really, really big

It was probably a great time to live … if you don't mind living like a Neanderthal!

You're probably wondering what would be served at one of these ancient parties. Well, for starters they would definitely put together a batch of Chef Dan's Qafzeh Quiche and a salad topped with his special Hybrid Dressing. We want to keep it light, of course, since there's still some more evolving to do, and it can be dangerous to mutate on a full stomach.

Study Questions

1. Explain why it would have been better if university deans went extinct instead of mammoths.

2. Why do you suppose that chins developed in modern humans? Does their presence always indicate the use of chin straps? Does this imply that Neanderthals engaged in violent team sports?

3. List five characteristics of the person sitting next to you that suggest that he or she is really a Neanderthal.

Qafzeh Quiche

9" pie shell—you may make this or buy one pre-made
6 large eggs
1 cup Half and Half
pinch of nutmeg
salt and pepper to taste
6 oz. crab meat (I like snow crab, but blue or any other will do)
1 lb. asparagus
1/2 lb. shredded Swiss cheese

Blanch the asparagus in boiling water for about one minute and then shock it in ice water. Cut off the tips about 1/2 inch below the head. Place these into the pie shell with the crabmeat. Save the rest of the asparagus for soup or just eating as you please. Cover the asparagus and crabmeat with the cheese.

In a mixing bowl put the eggs and Half and Half and whisk together. Add the salt, pepper, and nutmeg and pour over the asparagus, crab, and cheese. Place the quiche on a cookie sheet and bake in a 350-degree oven for about thirty minutes. Lightly shake the quiche to see if it is done. If the center wiggles it is not quite finished. When it is firm, then take it out and let it cool for 10 minutes. Serve warm with fruit or salad.

Hybrid Dressing

1/2 cup red wine vinegar
1-1/2 cups walnut oil (this is the best but you may substitute olive oil)
2 tsp. chopped shallots
1 tbs. Dijon mustard
1 tsp. sugar
salt and fresh ground pepper to taste
1 tbs. fresh chopped basil

    Combine all ingredients and let stand for 2 hours so the flavors blend.
Serve on your favorite salad.

Been using the same tools for the last 1.5 million years?

NEW !

Blade

it cuts things !

now with retouching !

from Mousterian Industries

The Definition of "Modern" Homo sapiens (Part 2)

So, our ancestors started looking modern about 100,000 years ago but still acted like Neanderthals. When do we start to see evidence of modern behavior? To answer this question we have to turn to the archaeological record. This is a relief because archaeologists tend to be, on average, much smarter than physical anthropologists.

Keep in mind that we're still in the Paleolithic—this is before the age of pottery and well before any use of metals. People were still very mobile, moving around fairly large areas on a seasonal basis. And it is well before any notion of farming or herding was developed, so we're still just hunter-gatherers. In a sense, things are still pretty primitive. But unlike the small biological changes that mark the rise of modern Homo sapiens, the behavioral or technological changes from the Middle to the Upper Paleolithic, which takes place around 40,000 years ago, are really dramatic. And most important for us, we now have a whole new set of recipes.

The Upper Paleolithic has many interesting features that distinguish it from earlier periods, including new types of stone tools, bone tools, art, and architecture. You're not going to believe this, but one new kind of stone tool is a chisel. Yes, that's right—a chisel. And if that does not impress you, just imagine this—real spear heads made of bone or stone appear at this time. No more hunting with sharpened sticks, no way—we're modern now! You can see that archaeologists are good at coming up with important criteria for defining modern behavior, unlike those physical anthropologists who simply look at bumps on a skull.

Perhaps the most dramatic difference between the Middle and Upper Paleolithic is the explosion in artistic expression. Before the Upper Paleolithic there are only a few isolated objects found here and there that could be interpreted as art only if you closed one eye and crossed the other—a scratched pebble or some bones with intriguing cutmarks on them, etc. Now we have the real McCoy—painted caves, with plenty of drawings of animals and mystical signs, bone carvings of animals, and decorated tools. Even a culture-less dolt like myself can appreciate these things as art, and I don't know the difference between a Remboir and a Von Go.

Upper Paleolithic painted caves are a real treat, though, and you have to plan on visiting some the next time you are in southwest France. A lot of people think that the art in these caves were simply wall decorations, but this is clearly not the case since the art tends to be found way, way back in the cave (sometimes up to a half-mile from the entrance). If you've ever been in a deep cave, you know that no one would really live back there. For one thing, it's dark. And damp. And spooky. In fact, there are usually no real signs of habitation, like artifacts or fires, back where the art itself is found. It's as if the people wandered back in there in order to put up the drawings where nobody else could see them. These were true artists who were not interested in crass commercialism.

Now, we could speculate forever as to why they did this. Was it a kind of magic ritual in which people drew animals on the walls in order to ensure the fertility of these animals? Was it a kind of hunting magic? Was it a totemic initiation ceremony of some sort? Or was it just a psychological urge to go back to the womb? Yes, it's true—people have suggested that last one. OK, now look: we all have urges to return to the safety of the womb, and given the stress of working with my academic colleagues, this particular urge strikes me quite often. But it never has occurred to me to take along some crayons and draw pictures in there!

What's amazing is that until just recently we never found one skeleton of a lost person in any of these caves. We do find footprints all the time in these caves, but bodies are extreme-

78

ly rare. Now remember, they were going way, way, way back in these caves with only torches or oil lamps. Nowadays people get lost in caves all the time—and even with modern spelunking equipment. You would think that 25,000 years ago they would have had an even riskier time. Maybe they wore some kind of Paleolithic homing beacons or something, or maybe they could just scream really, really loud. Who knows?

But recently, in a cave in southern France called Cussac, several individuals were found—not deliberately buried, but more or less intact on the surface. The cave itself has many spectacular engravings and it's easy to imagine that after a hard day's decorating, this small group of artists just got lost and ended up spending the rest of the Paleolithic there. On the other hand, and don't tell him I said this, it could also be that they tried out one of Chef Dan's recipes.

Painted caves are, of course, a big tourist industry in France today. In fact, in its heyday, one of the most famous of these sites, Lascaux (lass-KO), had up to 10,000 people a day go through it. This caused major problems, of course, since all of those breathing, sniffling, sweating, coughing tourists tended to warm up and moisturize the air to the point where mold began to form and destroy the paintings. The only way to solve the problem was to close down the site to tourists. But, in a bold move, the French made an exact replica a few hundred meters away from the original cave and hired an artist to recreate the drawings. This replica is called Lascaux II: The Fake. Now the problem is that so many people visit the fake Lascaux that the same problems are happening there. I can't wait until they close it down (except to important scholars like me) and open up Lascaux III: Bigger, Better, and Even More Profitable.

Chef Dan thought that you might like to recreate those long-lost days by decorating your own cave, uh, I mean, cake. Remember to include lots of deer, horses, bulls, and mammoths.

Study Questions

1. To the average person, going deep inside a cave to decorate it might seem a little stupid. Explain why, however, such behavior is only the tip of the proverbial iceberg when it comes to how modern humans act. Would a Neanderthal do such a foolish thing? (Hint: No).

2. Explain why chisels are the hallmark of modern behavior. Once you figure this out, publish a paper on it so that the rest of us will know.

81

Upper Paleolithic Cake

1/2 lb. + 2 oz. butter
1 lb. + 4 oz. sugar
1/2 tsp. salt
6 medium eggs
1 lb. flour
1-1/2 tbs. baking powder
2 tsp. vanilla
1-1/4 cups milk

In a mixer, cream the butter, sugar, and salt together with the paddle attachment until smooth. A hand mixer will do fine. Add the eggs one at a time, beating until smooth and creamy. Add the flour and baking powder and incorporate. Finally, put in the remaining ingredients and mix to a smooth batter.

Pour the batter into three 9-inch round cake pans that have been buttered and floured. Bake at 350 degrees until golden and a toothpick comes out clean. This will take about 30 minutes. Remove from oven and cool.

Buttercream Paint

12 oz. butter
4 oz. shortening
2 lbs. confectioners sugar
whites from 2 medium eggs
1 tsp. lemon juice
1-1/2 tsp. vanilla

Cream these together until smooth. Use food coloring if you like but keep in mind that you want a light neutral color so you can paint on the cake. Ice the cooled cakes with this and stack on top of each other.

For the paint, I recommend you use all shortening and no butter, or a pound of shortening. This will help the art stay formed on the canvas since butter would make it too soft for decorations (but it is wonderful for the base). Add whatever colors you like for the paint. The originals were black and dark red but we have more options for our cave art, and you might prefer to use food colors and not manganese, ochre, and charcoal like our ancestors did. Using a pastry bag and some decorating tips, draw whatever animals that you like the best!

83

Upper Paleolithic Industries of France

The greatest thing about the Upper Paleolithic, from my point of view, is that we are able to come up with a lot more esoteric names for different cultures. Names that are difficult to pronounce, difficult to spell, and difficult to remember. In other words, they are great for tests. Just to give you an idea of what I'm talking about, let's look at the Upper Paleolithic sequence in Europe.

Beginning about 40,000 years ago, a new group enters Europe—the Aurignacian (or-ig-NA-shun). There is some evidence that this culture originates in the hilly areas of Iraq, Iran, and Turkey, but it quickly spreads out into neighboring areas and seems to replace the Middle Paleolithic. In Europe, the spread of the Aurignacian probably represents the arrival of modern-looking humans there, and there is some debate (oh no, not more debate!) as to whether they killed off the Neanderthals, interbred with them, or just out-reproduced them. There's the sex and violence thing again, which just shows that we have really reached our own lofty position in human evolution. Actually, some anthropologists argue that language is what gave the Aurignacian people their competitive edge. I've put many students to sleep with my lectures, and so it's easy to understand how this new weapon could be used quite effectively when colonizing a new continent.

At about 27,000 years ago, the Aurignacian is replaced by a new culture called the Gravettian (gra-VET-ee-un). The Gravettian people came up with a number of interesting things, including houses made of mammoth (that is, really big) bones—which must have really stank

during hot weather—and the famous Venus figurines. These Venus figurines, which are always full-figured females, usually emphasize girth at the expense of anything else.

At about 21,000 years ago the Solutrean (so-LOO-tree-un) came on the scene in France. For Paleolithic archaeologists, the Solutrean represents one of the early pinnacles of flintknapping technology, producing incredibly well-made bifacial points, some of them almost 18 inches long. These are called "Laurel Leaf Points" by archaeologists, because they look just like the bay leaves we use in cooking.   Could it be that they made these as part of their own version of a Stone Age cookbook? Is it a coincidence also that this culture is named after the site of Solutré, which is located in the heart of the region famous for Pouilly-Fuissé wine? I don't believe in coincidences. These Solutreans were obviously busy creating exceptional gastronomic delights even way back then.

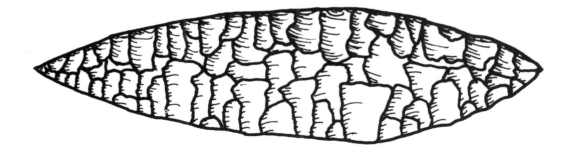

On the other hand, I'd like to point out that it is pure coincidence that most Paleolithic sites in France happen to be located in those regions known either for wine or gastronomy. I for one would never pick a site just because it's located right next to a good restaurant—usually there have to be other amenities as well. Personally, I prefer to excavate sites that are (a) close to the road so that there is no hiking required to get to them; (b) located out of the sun (yes, it gets hot in France during the summer); and (c) easy to dig (no big rocks or trees that have to be removed). Chef Dan does all our cooking and so who needs restaurants?

The last of the Upper Paleolithic cultures in France is called the Magdelenian (mag-da-LIN-ee-un), which begins about 18,000 years ago and lasts until the end of the Ice Ages at about 10,000 years ago. This culture is probably most famous for its artistic expression, seen both in painted caves, such as Lascaux, or in their decorated tools and weapons in bone. The Magdelenian was thriving during much of the coldest parts of the last Ice Age and in many ways resembled modern Eskimo culture. Their bone harpoons were used to catch salmon and they also relied heavily on reindeer, especially a species known as Reindeerus rodulfensis (now extinct except in the extreme north), which had an especially bright, red nose. You know—I wonder if that's what they used to light their way through those caves?

OK, I'm about out of breath here listing off all of these new cultures. What a difference, though, from the preceding Lower and Middle Paleolithic, where we can go hundreds of thousands of years with hardly any change at all. Now things start changing all the time and the number of archaeological culture names starts multiplying like rabbits. Not long after this people start settling down into villages (the start of the Neolithic, or New Stone Age), and eventually cities begin to form and people become literate (OK, some people). In just a blink of an eye we have the beginnings of the great civilizations, the industrial revolution, and finally, we have us. Oh great, and I wanted to end this on a happy note.

I know what will cheer you up, though. Try some of Chef Dan's fantastic Upper Paleolithic recipes.

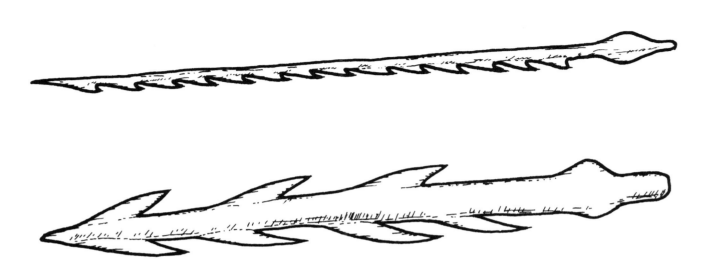

Study Questions

1. Explain why all of these Upper Paleolithic groups have names that end in –ian.
2. With the exception of indoor plumbing and the few years when the Beatles were together, have things really improved since the Paleolithic?
3. What is your favorite Paleolithic period and why?

Aurignacian Crustaceans

1 lb. shrimp, peeled
10 cloves garlic, chopped
2 shallots, chopped
1/2 cup flour
1 bunch fresh parsley, chopped
3 cups white wine
1 red bell pepper, diced fine
1/2 stick whole butter, cut into pieces
2 tbs. olive oil
salt and pepper to taste
1 lb. of your favorite pasta (I like sun-dried tomato linguine, but you may use basil pasta or plain or whatever you like)

Cook the pasta ahead of time and cool. Set this aside for later. Heat the olive oil in a sauté pan on high heat. Dust the shrimp in the flour and sauté in the oil until lightly browned. Add the peppers, garlic, and shallots and sauté for about 30 seconds. Pour in the wine and reduce it by half. This means you cook it until it evaporates and leaves you with half the original volume. Then turn the burner down to medium.

At this point season with the salt and pepper and sprinkle in the parsley flakes. Then put the butter pieces into the pan and shake it into the sauce. You will notice that this thickens the sauce, which is good. Toss in the pasta to heat it and serve immediately. You may choose to add or subtract from the amount of garlic depending on your taste.

Solutrean Reindeer Steaks

If you have a barbecue grill it will be the best for this. If not the oven will do nicely.

reindeer steaks- however many you like. You pick the size.
1–2 cups red wine
1 cup olive oil
3 tbs. shallots, chopped
1/2 cup fresh herbs, chopped
3 tbs. Dijon mustard
fresh ground pepper to taste
salt to taste

     The kinds of herbs you use are up to you. I like basil, tarragon, rosemary, and thyme. You may use anything you like or any combination. Since game meat is pretty lean (not as much fat) marinating it helps to make it more tender.

     Put the red wine, olive oil, shallots, herbs, mustard, and fresh-ground pepper into a container big enough to hold the steaks. Mix it well and add the steaks, being sure to coat them with the marinade. Cover and refrigerate for 4 hours, turning the steaks in the marinade once.

     Heat up the grill and remove the steaks from the marinade. Cook them on each side until desired doneness. Depending on size it will take 4–6 minutes per side to get them medium rare to medium. Less if they are thin and more if they are thick. Salt to taste and serve right away. You may use the rest of the marinade to baste them as they cook.

Gravettian Gumbo

2 lbs. chicken breasts
1 lb. Andouille sausage or
      Polish sausage cut into bite-sized pieces
1 cup flour
1/2 cup vegetable oil
1 medium-sized onion finely chopped
2 green bell peppers, seeded and finely chopped
2 stalks celery finely chopped
1 bulb garlic peeled and minced
2 quarts chicken stock
2–3 cups cooked converted rice
1 can diced tomatoes
1 package sliced frozen okra (about one cup is enough)

For seasoning:
2 tbs. granulated garlic
1 tsp. basil
2 tbs. granulated onion
1 tsp. oregano
salt to taste
1/2 tsp. thyme
1/4–1/2 tsp. black pepper
2 bay leaves
dash of Tabasco
1/8–1/4 tsp. cayenne pepper
1/8–1/4 tsp. white pepper

Heat a heavy stockpot with about half of the oil in it. I like a cast iron one here too. Dredge the chicken breasts in the flour and sauté them in the hot oil until browned. Remove from oil and cut into bite-sized pieces when cool. Add the sausage, onions, celery, peppers, and about 2–3 tbs. of the flour to the oil. You may need to add a bit more of the oil at this stage to keep it all from sticking.

Cook on medium heat until the onions are translucent and the flour starts to turn reddish-brown, but keep stirring so it does not scorch. Add the spices minus the salt and the minced garlic and stir for about 20–30 seconds, being careful not to burn the garlic. Add the tomatoes and the stock and bring to a boil. Turn to a simmer. Add the okra and the chicken and adjust the seasoning. Also feel free to add any of your favorite seafood to this gumbo if you desire. I like crawfish, shrimp, scallops, mussels, and clams. I play with the seasoning until I get it just right. The measurements I give are a starting point depending on how hot you like it. When you get it the way you like it add the cooked rice and bring back to a simmer. Add a dash of Tabasco and serve in a big bowl with lots of French bread.

While this is not my coveted secret gumbo recipe that some of you may have tried, it is a good one, and I am sure you will enjoy it. My secret gumbo recipe is pretty complicated and consequently yummy, driving many to fits of evolution-accelerating behavior, and I am not sure it is appropriate for a family book such as this.

Magdelenian Mammoth Meatballs

2 lbs. ground beef
1 small onion diced fine
1 stalk celery diced fine
1 small carrot diced fine
3 cloves garlic minced
2 tbs. olive oil
2 eggs
2 cups bread crumbs
2 tbs. tomato paste
salt and pepper to taste

1 tsp. basil
1 tsp. oregano
1/2 tsp. thyme
1 tsp. rosemary
1 tsp. garlic powder
1 tsp. onion powder
1 tsp. parsley flakes
1/2 tsp. marjoram
3 beef bouillon cubes

Sauté the onion, celery, and carrots in the oil until the onion is translucent. Add the garlic for the last 30 seconds and then set aside to cool. When cool place all the ingredients in a mixing bowl and mix together or in a stand mixer with a paddle. Form into balls by rolling in your hands. Be sure to make them big—they should be mammoth, after all. Plus they will shrink a bit when you cook them.

Line them up on a cookie sheet (make sure it is one with a lip on it or you will have grease all over your oven) and bake them in a 350-degree oven for about 10–15 minutes (being careful not to overcook them). Add them to your favorite sauce and enjoy. I like them in marinara sauce with pasta. Or try them in barbecue sauce for an appetizer. They also make great Swedish meatballs.

A Prehistory Dinner Party

Now that you know all about human evolution and the kinds of food that our furry and small-brained ancestors were enjoying, you are probably eager to put your knowledge to some good use. A really delicious idea would be to invite some of your close friends over for dinner and treat them to some of Chef Dan's recipes. But we can make it more than just good tasting—we can make it fun and intellectual (oh boy!) at the same time by organizing the dinner according to the tempo of human prehistory. In other words, we'll have the whole evening represent the span of human evolution—from Lucy to the present—and the various courses will represent major evolutionary milestones along the way. The fun part will be to serve each course at the appropriate moment as significant things happened in prehistory. In other words, a kind of gastronomic timeline.

Let's plan this out. Suppose that we have our guests arrive at 7:00, and we would like them to leave at 10:00. That gives us three full hours for all of human prehistory, which means that each minute of the dinner party will represent 25,000 years.

Here we go:

1. The beginning of the dinner party will represent the origins of the human line, as represented by *Australopithecus afarensis*. Our guests arrive promptly at 7:00 (that is, 4.5 million years ago) and, being gracious hosts, we seat them and begin serving cocktails. We're going to sit and chat for a while until the next major

event, which will be the beginnings of stone tools. It would be good if you like these people, because you are going to have to sit, drink, and make small talk for a long, long time. You can't hurry evolution, you know. The last time someone tried to do that we ended up with Dan Quayle as Vice-President.

2. Once everyone is settled, we can bring out some of Chef Dan's hors d'oeuvres, such as his Laetoli Trail Mix or a Mousterian hors d'oeuvres tray. If we plan on bringing them out at the time that corresponds to the first tools, then serve them promptly at 8:20. Don't worry—you'll have plenty of time for your guests to enjoy several helpings of these tasty tidbits.

3. At exactly 9:00 ask those who can still walk or crawl to come to the table. Tell your guests that their moving "Out of Living Room" represents the first movement of *Homo erectus/ergaster/antecessor* Out of Africa.   This will excite them tremendously and they'll probably hoot with joy. Once they're at the table serve up a gésier salad—they will love it—and regale them with stories of the dangers faced by those intrepid pioneers.

4. At 9:50 we're ready for the main course, with Confit de Canard, Pommes de Terres Gésier Salad, and salsify. The event we're talking about is, of course, the beginnings of Neanderthals at about 250,000 years ago. Yes, I know—we only have ten minutes left so you're going to have to get them to eat quickly. This should not be a problem, since your guests will be very hungry by this time and they will probably want to eat something substantial to help soak up all of the alcohol you've been serving.   It might save time if, instead of serving the main course on individual plates, you instead let your guests eat directly from a communal pot, digging in with long-handled wooden trowels (in keeping with an archaeological theme) or maybe with just their hands. Archaeologists call this "eating in the way of Neanderthals."

5. Get ready to serve your Pech de l'Azé Peche Melba to commemorate the origins of modern-looking humans. Let's see, that happens at about 100,000 years ago, which would be four minutes before the end of the dinner party. So, serve up the dessert at 9:56.   Give them a couple of seconds to admire your culinary talents, and then let them loose on it.

6. Finally we get to the beginnings of the Upper Paleolithic—when people really begin to act like people —at 9:58 and 24 seconds, and we'll use this time to savor a nice cup of coffee or tea. Well, actually, since you've only got 1.5 minutes left, you might want to just throw the coffee or tea at them. Make sure it's not too hot because you'll want to avoid lawsuits. Warning: if one of your guests prefers a cognac instead of coffee, make sure that there are no open flames in the room— or you may end up with a big helping of "Guest Flambée" on your hands.

7. A good host will usually give a healthy yawn to signal that the evening is drawing to a close. Just for fun, let's time this to correspond to the origins of settled village life, which began at about 8,000 years ago. In our scale, that yawn should come at 9:59 and 28 seconds—plenty of time for them to get the message and realize that you want them out of there.

8. Let's start pushing them out the door just at the time of the origins of the first cities in Mesopotamia, or at 9:59 and 36 seconds. Remember, each second is actually over 400 years, so you could try to point out other major historic events as each of them is leaving ("George, you represent the building of the Great Pyramids; Sally, you are the beginning of the Christian era; Uncle Irving, you are Atilla the Hun," etc.). The last one, just a half-second before 10:00, can be Thomas Jefferson.

9. As the door slams shut at exactly 10:00, we finally come right up to the present. It's at this time that you realize you'll probably never see those people again.

Salad de Gesier/ Confit de Canard
Pommes de terres du Perigord

This is a dinner party for 4. If you would like to serve more you will have to remember your multiplication tables. The recipe for the confit was taught to me by my good friends at the Delpayrat hotel in the south of France and is the way they make it for their guests in the authentic French way.

2 whole ducks—you should be able to find
   these at the local market.
   If not ask the butcher.
kosher salt
salad greens. I like spring greens. Pick what you like.
1/2 cup walnuts
Hybrid Vinaigrette found earlier in this book

8 cherry tomatos cut in half
1-1/2 lbs. new potatoes (golden new potatoes)
wood chips. I like hickory. Check the hardware store
1 head garlic
2 shallots
1 bunch fresh chopped parsley
salt and fresh ground pepper to taste

    The first thing you need to do is plan ahead. This preparation will take 2, yes 2, days.

    Remove the gizzards from the duck and set aside. You may throw out the livers or save them for another recipe. Remove the breasts from the duck and then remove the leg and thigh in one piece. If you do not feel as though you can do this, then ask your butcher to do it for you. Be sure you ask him to save the gizzards for the Gésier Salad. Save the carcass for a good stock. If you do not make your own stock then you may throw them away. It will, however, be a shame.

    Place the legs and thighs in a plastic container and salt them individually with kosher salt or sea salt. Also add any remaining fat from the duck carcass. You may salt fairly liberally. Cover them with a lid or plastic wrap. Put the breasts in a separate container without the salt. Refrigerate the legs and thighs for two days. Put the gizzards in a small bowl and salt liberally as well. Wrap and put in the fridge for two days.

    You may decide to smoke the breasts ahead of time so you don't have to worry about it on the day of the party. I line a pan with foil and put the breast on a rack that fits inside the pan. Soak the wood chips for about an hour in cold water.

(continued on next page)

Drain the water and place them in the bottom of the pan. Cover the pan and place on a burner on medium heat. This will start the wood to smoking. Be sure you use a well-ventilated area so your house doesn't fill with smoke or better yet, use your gas grill outside. Place the breasts on the rack and season with a bit of salt and pepper. When the pan is smoking place the breasts in the pan and cover. Smoke them in the pan for 5–10 minutes only. Be careful not to overdo it or you'll lose the flavor of the duck. Remove from the smoking pan and finish in a 350-degree oven until about medium rare to medium. Remove and cool overnight.

Now, on the day of the party remove the legs and thighs from the refrigerator and rinse them. Place them in a stockpot and cover them with water. Put it on the range and bring to a boil. Turn down to a simmer and cook them approximately 2 hours. They will be very tender but not falling apart. Remove them and cool. Place some of the liquid in a saucepan and do the same process for the gizzards. Skim the remaining fat from the thighs and legs and set aside. This will be used to brown the ducks and cook the potatoes. You may choose to reserve the liquid minus the fat from the legs and thighs to use for stock or to add to the stock you are making with the carcass. When the gizzards are cooked remove them and cool. Discard this liquid.

Blanch the potatoes in boiling water until tender but firm. Cool them and slice about 1/4 inch thick. Chop the garlic and shallots fine as well as the parsley.

Now you may be asking how this mess comes together to make a meal. Well, let's tackle the Gésiers Salad first. Slice the gizzards and sauté them in a bit of the reserved duck fat. Place the greens on your salad plate and slice the smoked duck breasts very thin and arrange around the outside edge of the greens. This will be served cold while the gésiers are warm. Place the Gésiers on the top. Sprinkle with some walnuts and garnish with the tomatoes. Drizzle the vinaigrette over the top and serve with some good crunchy baguette bread. This is a great appetizer/salad for your guests. Don't tell them what the gizzards are until afterwards because Americans tend to get a bit squeamish about these delicious items.

For the main course you need to heat a cast-iron skillet or griddle and put some of the reserved fat in it. Brown the potatoes in the fat being careful not to turn them too much or they will not brown too well. At the end add the garlic and shallots. They will burn if you put them in too early. Season with salt and pepper and sprinkle parsley flakes over them. In a separate pan heat some reserved fat and brown off the legs and thighs. This will heat them through as well. They are cooked so they just need to get up to temperature and brown.

This is one of those exotic meals that will please even the pickiest of eaters. The Confit literally melts in your mouth and the potatoes complement nicely. Be sure to serve this with a nice bottle of red wine. I like the wines from the Bordeaux region for this one, such as a good Pecharment.

FAQs about Prehistory

I'm asked a lot of questions (actually, Frequently Absurd Questions) about human evolution and such. Since it's impossible to cover everything in a brief, but highly entertaining narrative—ok, a long and not-so-entertaining narrative—I thought that it might be nice to share some of questions with you.

Q: Are people really descended from monkeys?
A: Absolutely not. Monkeys are a whole line of primates that differ in many ways from apes, and we are actually a kind of ape. In fact, we're most closely related to chimpanzees. It does seem likely, however, that our last roundup of Presidential candidates came from completely unrelated life forms, namely squid.

Q: How do you choose which site to dig?
A: I personally like to look for sites that have the most amount of stuff in them, and I especially like sites where there are human remains. This is because finding a new fossil human is the quickest and easiest way to achieve fame and glory. So far, unfortunately, this approach has not worked for me, which is why I've resorted to writing cookbooks to fund my research.

Q: Who was Cro-Magnon Man?

A: Cro-Magnon Man was a member of our famous group—modern Homo sapiens—who was found in the French village of Les Eyzies. He probably lived about 27,000 years ago. His family, however, still lives in the area and, until recently, ran a very nice hotel there.

Q: I have a lump in my left leg, just below the knee. Could it be dangerous?

A: Don't ask me—ask a "real" doctor!

Q: What site are you working at now?

A: I'm working at a very nice site called Pech de l'Azé, which is located in the Dordogne Valley near the town of Sarlat. The excavation is co-directed by my colleague, Professor Shannon McPherron. You can visit our website at www.oldstoneage.com.

Q: Can I contribute money to help fund your excavations?

A: This question comes up a lot, and the answer is: Of course. Please make the check payable to The University of Pennsylvania Museum of Archaeology and Anthropology. If the donation is large enough we may be persuaded to name a new Paleolithic tool type after you (just imagine site reports in the future: "At the Mousterian site of Combe-Canard, we found 124 George and Ethel Schwartz scrapers, 37 Chuck and Doris Smith denticulates, and 16 YOUR-NAME-HERE bifaces.").

Q: If I give you money, can I visit you?

A: Yes, we welcome visitors. Unfortunately, the site will be closed on those particular days when you can come over.

Q: How did you become an archaeologist?
A: I bought a shovel.

Q: Isn't it true that you and all of those other pseudo-scientists like art historians, psychologists, sociologists, and theater critics are just wasting taxpayer money?
A: I couldn't agree more about those other fields. Paleolithic archaeology is, however, of utmost importance to our National Security and the health of our population. In fact, there will be another Ice Age in several thousand years, and we'd be in trouble if we didn't know how our ancestors coped with it.

Q: Why did I waste my money on this stupid book?
A: Ha-ha-ha-ha-ha-ha-ha-ha-ha-ha-ha-ha.